1099 Compliance

What every Accounts Payable professional must know about it

A fully revised and updated 2022 edition

Costa Levi Perepeliza

(CPA)

New York, 2022

Edited by Moises Nederlander, PhD

New York 2022

Barnegat Lighthouse Business Publications

Eight Edition

Copyright © 2022 by C Levi Perepeliza

Originally published in April 2013

Barnegat Lighthouse Business Publications
P.O.BOX 33695   Bay Ridge NY 11209

Book design and production: Emily-Liz Daniels / Barnegat Lighthouse Business Publications

Library of Congress Cataloging - .in - Publication Data

Perepeliza, Costa Levi, 1969 –

1099 Compliance - What every Accounts Payable professional must know about it

Includes appendix

ISBN – 13: 978-1484160688

ISBN – 10: 1484160681

This book is dedicated to Iryne and our children

Other books by Costa Levi P., CPA

Accounts Payable in the 21st Century Business
Environment

Nonresident Alien Tax Compliance

Content

Back to the Future – the 1099-NEC is back!

Last used for filing for year 1982, the 1099-NEC is back to use for filing for year 2020 and after.

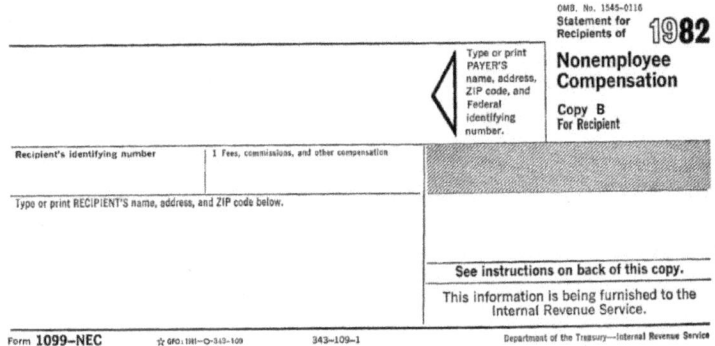

Meet the new/old 1099-NEC, *non-employee compensation* reporting form which is due to all recipients and the IRS by January 31st . Why all the trouble with forms changing?! Consultants payments is an income area with plenty of 'freedom' to avoid or manipulate with taxes, FICA liabilities, and tax refund fraud. Think, when you get your paycheck (reported on W-2 form), all kinds of taxes are taken from it – Federal, State, Local, MTA (for New York City, MTA tax (to sponsor the sleepy Metro Transit Authority), unemployment, FICA.

The consultants' payments have no such oversight and control – consultants get paid full or 'gross' dollars, and then they reconcile and calculate, and pay the taxes due. It is not an assumption that some consultants avoid paying taxes – or the IRS would not be fine-tuning and tightening the 1099 process so much.

You may have noticed during your carrier that many W-9 consultants try their best not to submit the W-9, try to present themselves as not-reportable entities, or provide corporate type W-9 while requesting payments to be made to a person – you might have seen all this, I have. Or, in the days bygone, dispute the issued forms 1099-Misc after January 31, before your reported the amounts to the IRS. From my experience: the W-9 consultants are more agile and 'pushy' people than most of us – and many desire to reduce their tax liability – with you as an inadvertent accomplice… So, the IRS knows it all – and we are caught in the middle – reports to both consultants and the IRS are now due by January 31st, like it or not.

Bottomline: report to the IRS by the same date as you report it to the consultants, January 31st – ostensibly, to cancel the two month period (old, by March 31, to file electronically with the IRS) when the consultants, some, would bombard the AP Manager with the reasons why their reported 1099-MISC, Box 7 forms income should be cancelled. I've gone through those heated conversations, yes, I did.

Now there's more pressure on you – better not make a mistake when reporting to the Consultant and IRS at the same time, mistake which triggers a cancellation of the reported to the IRS by January 31 amount.

In some ideal and impeccable AP department, one will generate all 1099-NECs on January 2nd, mail them out to consultants – and allow a three-weeks periyod to hear back from the recipients for any type of 1099 error, before reporting to the IRS by January 31st. But then – the said ideal and impeccable AP would not have any errors in the 1099 reporting. I tried this in the past years – never worked. Because? At this same January time you are likely responsible for year-end reconciliations, closings, GL chart update, Concur mileage-rate updates, sales tax monthly, quarterly, semi-annual, annual, reporting, and other new ear great ideas implementation taking place.

OK, let's be positive and just talk about how we can run an orderly 1099 reporting season. Report $600 and more of the total service payments made. All in box 1. There is only one box to report payments – Box 1. Federal Income Tax withheld goes in Box 4 – remember the B-notice? The back-up tax withholding from those who don't correct their SSN/EIN is reported here – I know of no single instance of back-up tax collected (22 years on active AP duty).

It's there is, when we are talking about transitioning old Box 7 on 1099-MISC into 1099-NEC. Only nonemployee compensations get reported on 1099-NEC. Legal services are also reported in Box 1 on 1099-NEC – the corporate exemption does not apply to the legal firms. Gross judgement awards proceeds paid to attorneys or legal firm remain assigned Box 10 of 1099-MISC.

You will likely need a few 1099-MISC forms still; report on form 1099-MISC: (by box number) 1 – Rents, 2 – Royalties, 3 – Other Income, 5 – Fishing boat proceeds, 6 – Medical and Healthcare payments for services, not insurance payments, are porting in box 6, 1099-MISC – the corporate exemption does not apply to medical service providers.

Box 1, 1099-NEC, due on or before February 1ˢᵗ (Sec 6071-c) to both recipients and the IRS. Recipients get paper forms (ITIN can be truncated), IRS gets paper only under 250 forms count, and electronic over 250, while e-filing is strongly advised for any number of IRS reports. No truncation of tax IDs allowed when reporting to the IRS. Checking box VOID will make IRS scanner skip the marked form, no matter what information is on it.

(IRS instructions)

Pursuant to Regulations section 301.6109-4, all filers of this form may truncate a recipient's TIN (social security number (SSN), individual taxpayer identification number (ITIN), adoption taxpayer identification number (ATIN), or employer identification number (EIN)) on payee statements. Truncation is not allowed on any documents the filer files with the IRS. A payer's TIN may not be truncated on any form

Payments to corporations (except legal and medical) are not reportable. Payments for merchandise, … freight, storage are not reportable. Payments to tax exempt organizations (governments and nonprofits) are not reportable. Payments made with credit card are not reportable by you (but the payment settlement entity (Sec 6050W)). Non-service scholarships made to US tax residents are not reportable.

I do not include with service payments any reimbursements made to the service-providers. I report 'clean' service amounts. The alternative is to report 'gross' and let the recipients deduct the reimbursement amounts as a part of their itemized deduction process.

Let us examine the 'incomplete' year on form 1099-NEC – 20___ - you can now use forms for multiple years. This is very nice of the IRS – I used to buy more forms, and always have left over copies – not anymore. *Form 1099-MISC, Form 1099-NEC, and these instructions have been converted from an annual revision to continuous use. Both the forms and instructions will be updated as needed.*

The rest of discussion in this book is dedicated to the filing details for form *1099-MISC, Miscellaneous Income and 1099-NEC, Nonemployee compensation*. 1099-NEC is becoming the most used form by the Accounts Payable profession and the least elaborate form 1099 of all the variations of form 1099 (see listing of forms 1099 in the Appendix). There is no genuine need to read any books about, let's say, processing of form 1099-INT (Interest income); all, or almost all, you need to do when processing forms 1099-INT is to push the button called "Process form 1099-INT" on your banking computer keyboard before January 31st to get your system spit out thousands of 1099-INT forms with paid interest dollar figures filled in Box 1. Therefore, keep in mind that this book is mainly about processing of form 1099-NEC and to a lesser degree, 1099-MISC.

Make sure as to properly process the AP data during the year, and have forms W-9 for all payees, new or existing, on file. (I will talk about exceptions to the W-9 rule later in the book.) Have the payees' AP records populated with the tax ID numbers and the form of business ownership information. Then report cumulative for the reporting calendar year rents (Box 1), royalties (Box 2), prizes and awards, other income payments (Box 3), medical and health care payments (Box 6), gross judgement proceeds (not service payments) paid to attorneys (Box 10). Report nonemployee compensations (contractors, service providers, entertainers, speakers, caterers, drivers, couriers) payments in Box 1 of form 1099-NEC.

Report combined total for a year of $600 and above and at least $10 in royalties or interest

Practical advice !!! Check for staledated non-cashed checks issued to the service providers in the reporting year. If there are 'staledated' service checks, you must void them and run them through the 'escheat' process. However, the concept of 'income made available' does not apply to such checks as the recipient was ostensibly not in power to assume such income. Void these checks – they are staledated (again, in the 'escheat' area now – reissue or report to state, TBD) – and exclude them from the 1099 reporting. Do not include in this process check which are not-cashed, but not staledated: for the '180 days' check validity term, those checks issued in July-December.

Notice that 1099-Misc Box 7 (nonemployee compensation) got replace with 'payor made direct sales' check only box.

PAYER'S name, street address, city or town, state or province, country, ZIP or foreign postal code, and telephone no.		1 Rents $	OMB No. 1545-0115 2021 Form 1099-MISC	Miscellaneous Information
		2 Royalties $		
		3 Other income $	4 Federal income tax withheld $	Copy B For Recipient
PAYER'S TIN	RECIPIENT'S TIN	5 Fishing boat proceeds $	6 Medical and health care payments $	
RECIPIENT'S name		7 Payer made direct sales totaling $5,000 or more of consumer products to recipient for resale ☐	8 Substitute payments in lieu of dividends or interest $	This is important tax information and is being furnished to the IRS. If you are required to file a return, a negligence penalty or other sanction may be imposed on you if this income is taxable and the IRS determines that it has not been reported.
Street address (including apt. no.)		9 Crop insurance proceeds $	10 Gross proceeds paid to an attorney $	
City or town, state or province, country, and ZIP or foreign postal code		11 Fish purchased for resale $	12 Section 409A deferrals $	
Account number (see instructions)	FATCA filing requirement ☐	13 Excess golden parachute payments $	14 Nonqualified deferred compensation $	
		15 State tax withheld $ $	16 State/Payer's state no.	17 State income $ $

Form 1099-MISC   (keep for your records)   www.irs.gov/Form1099MISC   Department of the Treasury - Internal Revenue Service

I can't help by ask this: Why bother doing the 1099 reporting at all? Don't people keep track of their earnings and report on their own? Some people do, some people do not. Some people do not because they honestly forget, some people do not want, when possible, to report their income and incur tax liability. Yes, some people are ready and willing, if presented with the opportunity, to conceal their income, tax cheat! Some simply forget. And we know that reporting of income and tax collecting are important administrative functions that help to keep our country "going" and assure its continuous fiscal well-being. Fairness of the tax laws is a topic beyond the scope of this book.

The accounts payable department's part in the process is to follow the tax law, which simply requests to *report payments to recipients by January 31 payments for services and rents of (1) $600 or more made during calendar year to all non-corporate income recipients, (2)*

medical/health and legal payments made to all business entities, (3) gross royalty payments of $10 or more paid to non-corporate recipients for patents, copyrights, trade names and trademarks and (4) other 'passive income' payments.

Report all nonemployee compensation on form 1099-NEC, box 1, to recipients and the IRS (both electronically and on paper) by January 31st.

Reports non-NEC 1099 reportable income (rent, royalties, prizes, other income, 'fish') <u>to the IRS</u> by February 28 on paper, or March 31 electronically.

Now, I will take time to talk the "taxpayer conscience and moral responsibility" aspect of the reporting process. I do not assume that many people under-report their income – I know it. People desire to increase their discretionary income by reducing their taxes, often by not reporting their income. There is an ancient wisdom of not letting people come close to desirable but forbidden fruits; wisdom not to test an individual's moral strength by placing him in the proximity to the sinful tax irregularities opportunities.

So, here we come, guardian angels with the 1099 forms in hand, the watchmen of the American tax compliance system.

Forms 1099 reminds the recipients of income received and alerts the IRS to expect that income to be included on individuals' forms 1040. Therefore, beware, the 1099 processing and customer service will at times become more adversarial than informational engagement. Be strong! Strength comes from knowledge (in this book) and experience (not in this book).

A good news: you don't need to buy 1099-MISC or 1099-NEC forms on Amazon anymore – the IRS made fillable forms available online, copies B & C. IRS red form A (and summary form 1096) is not needed if you file with IRS electronically. You will need red (copy A) IRS from 1099-MISC or NEC and form 1096 for correction of already issued forms.

Note that any form with box Void checked will <u>not</u> be read by the IRS scanner (will not register with the IRS). Check box Corrected if correcting a previously issued form. To zero out a previously reported amount (I do not want to use word 'void'), check 1099 as 'corrected' and put zero dollars in the previously reported field. This is how I have done it for the past 22 years - it has always worked.

By the way, only report on Form 1099-MISC or 1099-NEC payments made in the course of your trade of business – personal payments need not be reported. I can't imagine issuing a 1099 to my plumber who did something major in the basement this year, and then calling him for a midnight pipe rupture this year – I guess, wisdom takes precedence over any tax law, lol.

Rents of $600 and over go to Box 1 of 1099-MISC. Often rent is paid by your employee, during travel, to a non-corporate recipient. In the old days, I demanded that all third-party reportable payments are made through the AP and not via the reimbursement process. While it may appear as a sound practice, it is very impractical. The third-party reporting is an acceptable practice if the information gathering rules are followed. The process has less control, indeed; you rely on someone else to make an inquiry with the rent collecting party (collecting the W-9 information) and have the information documented and provided to you.

Royalty payments of at least $10 made to non-corporate intellectual property rights holders are reported in Box 2 (1099-MISC). This is the box that my publishes fills with my fat publishing earnings - and sends that information to me.

Other Income, reported in Box 3 (1099-MISC), must not be used interchangeably with Nonemployee compensation (1099-NEC). Think of it as of 'passive income' vs. nonemployee compensation being an actively earned income. Income in Box 1 of 1099-NEC is a service-type income (subject to self-employment tax) which reported on line 12 of *Form 1040* (US Individual Income Tax Return, see Appendix) and requires completing and attaching of *Schedule C* (Profit and Loss from Business). The 1099-NEC 1040 reporting process is more complicated for the income recipient than the "Box 3" 1099-MISC 1040 reporting. There is of course no picking and choosing of what box and form to fill based on any preferences, you must follow the rules; but you need to be cognizant of what your reporting entails for the recipients. The 1099 is not a "just report correct amount in whatever box" approach and process.

Other Income (Box 3, 1099-MISC) may include prizes, awards, participant's fees, attendance fees, and other *passive* types of income. Keep in mind, that non-service scholarship or fellowship, which must be truly *non-service*, by definition, are not reported to the IRS and the recipients. This may sound odd as such scholarship and fellowship payments often amount to tens of thousands of dollars per year per student. But the truth is, they are not required to be reported to the US persons (US tax residents). Students, on their own, must include the "non-qualifying" portion of the scholarship or fellowship payments (for more information read Internal Revenue Section 117 in the Appendix) in their gross income.

Scholarship and fellowship grants that are taxable to the recipient because they are paid for teaching, research, or other services as a condition for receiving the grant are considered wages and must be reported on Form W-2. (IRS Instructions for Form 1099-Misc)

I've been asked many times by the recipients about the process of scholarship or fellowship reporting and always surprised them by advising to merely include the *non-qualifying portion of scholarship or fellowship* (funds paid to a student at a qualified educational organization and not used for tuition, fees, books, supplies and equipment required for attendance, IRC § 117) on line 21 of the US individual income tax return (form 1040).

All scholarship or fellowship grants paid to a nonresident alien, [including *Accountable Plan* travel reimbursements, which are considered additional scholarship or fellowship], regardless of the amounts paid (there is no minimum reporting threshold), is reported on form 1042-S. Term *Scholarship* is mostly used for undergraduate grants payments. Term *Fellowship* is used for graduate and post-graduate grants payments. Avoid using term *Stipend* – it is vague and often all-inclusive.

Starting with reporting year 2020, the most used 1099 form has been 1099-NEC, Nonemployee compensation, with which payments for independent services are reported. This is the information the IRS is most interested in. Processing 1099-NEC data at times may present you with a dilemma; service payments, when combined with travel reimbursements, can makes the total combined amount 1099-reportable (equal or more $600). A learned accountant knows that business expenses are accounted for on *Schedule C* and deducted from business income. The service fees amount taken separately, excluding the *Accountable Plan* business reimbursement that your company may have paid to a service provider, may alone not arise to the reporting threshold.

To report or not to report – that is the question. You will be correct following either approach. Practically, it is easier and less burdensome (and contentious) to separate service fees from *Accountable Plan* reimbursements and determine the report-ability solely on the total amount of service fees payments made to a contractor during a calendar year. There will be no phone calls from the service providers complaining about your reporting practices and demands for cancellation of processed form 1099. And you will have followed the tax law under with either approach.

There are two possible reasons why the recipients complain about this kind of borderline "service fees plus business expenses combined" reporting practice: filing of the personal tax return and Schedule C becomes more complicated. Second, those desiring to "optimize taxes" (i.e. conceal income) are put on the IRS's radar by the issued form 1099 and now the income must be accounted for. Practically, there will be fewer 1099 forms to file and tense phone calls to answer if you do not include business 'accountable plan' reimbursements in your 1099 calculations; it makes sense to me not to include the reimbursements in the Box 1 amounts – I have not been doing it.

It should be decided as your company's policy to choose the *gross* or the *net* approach; once selected, the approach must be followed across the board uniformly for all payees. Again – use the net method, even if it involves vetting out the accountable plan reimbursements from a vendor marked for 1099-NEC reporting (meaning, manual review and adjustment).

Report payments for medical and health care services to all business entities, including corporations, in Box 6 of 1099-MISC.

A special case in the 1099 process: reporting federal income taxes withheld. I haven not ever had any amount reported in that box. For accounts payable purposes, the back-up withholdings made from payments to the persons who have not furnished their W-9s to you. Remember an easy way out of the "No W-9 on file" situation – set up the 24% back-up tax withholding (new 2018-2025 rate) for the non-complying payees. Use it as a matter of fact tool – *I do not have your W-9 - I take 24% from your payments.* Practically speaking, the situation must not escalate to withholding the 24% tax. It is your leverage – use it to correct tax IDs when you review the CP-2100 B-Notice IRS letter! Who will not supply you a corrected SSN/EIN and get 24% taken?! And get on the IRS' radar?!

Remember, you only have the back-up tax leverage before a payment is made.

If the W-9 is not on-file and the 24% was not withheld, you must gross-up and pay the back-up tax on vendor's behalf to the IRS. Report the back-up withholding to the vendor and the IRS. If this sounds like a super-complicated process, it is. It is better in such cases to report income to the vendor and the IRS with no TIN and pay the IRS penalty, $250 per form, if you cannot show a reasonable cause. *Do not go into these woods – gross up, back-up tax – just don't pay, hold payments.*

If you have an incorrect, as noted by the IRS, TIN onFile, and cannot correct it, the 2nd TIN Not rule applies. I never used the rule – I just do not pay a business that does not answer my B-Notice letters with proper information – my own little 'grey area' rule. I use the TIN matching IRS tool to validate any B-notice responses.

2nd TIN Not.

You may enter an "X" in this box if you were notified by the IRS twice within 3 calendar years that the payee provided an incorrect TIN. If you mark this box, the IRS will not send you any further notices about this account.

However, if you received both IRS notices in the same year, or if you received them in different years but they both related to information returns filed for the same year, do not check the box at this time. For purposes of the two-notices-in-3-years rule, you are considered to have received one notice and you are not required to send a second "B" notice to the taxpayer on receipt of the second notice. See part N in the 2020 General Instructions

With all the good advices provided hitherto, I know full well that there are situations when there is so much pressure to make a payment promptly, ASAP. Your bosses want the payment made with no W-9 on file, "collect the W-9 later" – a management override situation. However, in the end, *you* will be responsible for properly reporting this and any other payment.

Here is a bit of good news for the 'no W-9 on-file situation, inherited or acquired. There are often ways to find tax IDs online. Well, sure not the SSNs, but EINs. Use as the key internet search these words: [company name], EIN, 401, SEC filing, affidavit, defendant, plaintiff, state filing, form 990. Many a time you will find the EIN is some obscure filing with a pensions fund, court, or state tax authorities. Match the number using the IRS ITIN Matching system to be sure.

Example: I just searched for "Dell Inc., 401" and found this EIN provided by some Brightscope website: 74-2487834.

A great site to find many EINs (not SSNs) is this, which is my Chrome browser home page these days:

https://eintaxid.com/

You will ask me: but how about the form of business ownership, what if it is a corporation? I will tell this – *forget about it*. Report all payments made to the vendor who refused to provide the W-9 (whatever the circumstances were, if you can't gross up, withhold backup tax, or hold payment under the special local circumstances), but you found the EIN for. If the vendor desires to set the record straight after receiving the 1099 – you will see the W-9 in the mail soon.

In August – October you get 'graded' by the IRS on your 1099 filing performance earlier in January – you get your report card – CP2100A. The IRS alerts you of the prior year's 1099 names and tax IDs discrepancies reported in January - on IRS letter/form CP-2100A. This is the time when *you* should prepare and send out the B-Notices, demanding your payees to update forms W-9. The B-Notice is also called Back Up Withholding Warning Notice.

It has never occurred in my practice that I demanded a corrected form W-9 from an active payee and was refused the information. You must begin 24% back-up tax withholding (new rate! Effective for years 2018-2025) from all payments to non-compliant payees after certain actions and deadlines described in Notice CP-2100A. If this tax withholding does not sound realistic, it is not. You will probably never have a case of back-up taxes collected and reported. For the payees, the trouble is not worth it.

When you have the 1099 data ready, complete the forms. Let your system do it, of course. The required fields are - your business name and address, your business tax ID, recipient's tax ID, recipient's name, address, account number (your internal payee account number – it comes in handy when/if the IRS communicates payee's information to you. Also, a must if filing multiple forms for the same payee – I do not know why/when someone would do it). Report amount or amounts in appropriate 1099 boxes. One 1099-MISC form may show more than one completed box for different income types paid to the same payee, there is no need to separate the 1099-MISC for that. Form 1099-NEC has only one box to complete. Will you issue two 1099-NEC forms if you buy fish (Box 1) and services (Box 1) from the same business? I do not know.

The tax ID number of the recipient may be "truncated", that is, shortened, for security purposes on paper forms (see proposed regulation §§1.6042-4(b) and 301.6109-4 (REG-148873-09)). You may not truncate any tax ID number on the IRS forms, paper or electronic.

Filing dates: Section 6071(c) requires you to file Form 1099-NEC on or before January 31, using either paper or electronic filing procedures. File Form 1099-MISC by February 28, if you file on paper, or March 31, if you file electronically.

1099-MISC information is reportable to the recipients by January 31st and to the IRS by February 28 on paper, and March 31 electronically.

No separate filing of form 1096 is required if filing with the IRS electronically. I use form 1096 when I send corrected forms to the IRS – there is no way around using paper when correcting a filed form. Most of times, there will be errors and discrepancies reported by the 1099 recipients for any high volume and diverse payment types 1099 process. The error rate depends on quality of the W-9 data collection and processing, complexity and variety of the payments your accounts payable department makes, accuracy of GL coding, and/or flagging transactions as 1099-reportable on the entry level.

Any correction on individual forms 1099 should be ideally made before you report the 1099 information to the IRS: first, the recipient does not get on the IRS' radar for "no good reason" (your erroneous reporting) and second, the correction will be included in your original reporting to the IRS. For the most contested type of 1099 income, now on 1099-NEC form, the only way to receive feedback is to send out individuals 1099-NEC forms in the first week on January, and review and process any feedback by the time your report to the IRS by January 31st.

Unless your 1099 process is very simple, transparent, and flawless, do not rush reporting to the too early before January 31. But watch the calendar! Do not be late with your filing! Get a filing confirmation from the *IRS Fire* website if you are able to upload the data file yourself (that is, your accounting system produces such data file) or get confirmation from the reporting third party. I use www.tax1099.com – the provider is ok with me, no plans to change it this year.

That is all there is to keep in mind when processing the Accounts Payable 1099 forms – NEC and MISC; the following chapters are mere icing on the cake, the details. But, as you know, the devil is in the details.

The new IRS requirement to report Nonemployee compensation (NEC) by January 31st to both Contractor and the IRS is a big change in the process, and now on a dedicated form – for those of us old enough and used to the old ways. The IRS wants to better tackle the income reporting. I believe the IRS wants to leave less or not time in between the individual reporting and the IRS reporting (previously there was a one or two-months period in between) to disallow any communication between the payees and the payers that results in 1099 cancellations.

No matter how we look at it, the 1099 reporting process now is shortened to just one month for all intense and purposes. A big change - not in the AP departments' favor. There is no time for a January ski vacation in the Aspen, CO for us Accounts Payable people anymore – the most complex 1099-NEC reporting must be fully completed in January, there is the 1042 reporting, Monthly, Quarterly, Semi-Annual, Annual sales tax reporting, and the last nail, the company fiscal year may end on December 31st, which makes the month of January a true helter-skelter. *Yes, it is…*

Let us discuss a couple of special 1099 cases. Double reporting: there is an instance when you must report the same amount twice. Payment to a deceased person's estate is one case - the FICA taxes are withheld in the year of death, the W-2 is filed and the gross paid after death amount is reported on 1099-MISC (box 3) – to get taxman the federal income tax portion. Any payment after year of death triggers no FICA withholding and no W-2 filing, but the gross amount is reported in Box 3 of 1099-MISC. Remember I said, Box 3 of 1099-MISC shows 'passive income'. Another double reporting is the case of remitting taxable claims for damages via the attorney – both the claimant (in Box 3) and the attorney (box 14) must be issued forms 1099-MISC.

An interesting ruling about Foreign agricultural workers, which I never noticed, or it appeared for the first time in the 1099 reporting guide for year 2020: *Report in Box 3 compensation of $600 or more paid in a calendar year to an h-2A visa agricultural worker who did not give you a valid TIN. You must also withhold federal income tax under the backup withholding rules (24%).*

Form W-9

An efficient and tax compliant 1099 processing begins with requesting from all new payees and processing forms W-9. Some business collect current form W-9 for all payees with no exception. There's no need to do it, unless a vendor changes the business ownership or tax exemption status. So, no need to collect the most recent IRS version of the W-9 (October 2018) must be completed by all: only changes in the existing on file information, or additional FATCA requirements must be obtained from the vendors.

Request a properly completed form W-9 (with few exception) from every new payee that you make payments to. I frequently use the word *payee* and not *vendor* since it is an all-inclusive, businesses and individuals, AP term.

Non-US tax residents do not complete form W-9. Do not collect W-9s from government agencies. If I realize that there is a non-profit vendor in the system with no W-9 on file, I will request the form. Or I may decide to spend a minute finding the EIN on the web. This is a practical life approach that balances the request to have the EIN on file and knowledge that no 1099 reporting is required. You can find a tax ID for any non-profit company; enter search words *Name, 990 filing, financial statements, pdf.* Search for **Red Cross EIN** and see what happens – voila, ETIN is right there for you. I use this site to find EINs https://eintaxid.com .

I also do not collect the W-9 for accountable plan reimbursement payments. But be careful as your current reimbursement payee may reappear later as a contractor for which there will be an existing payee ID in the AP system with no tax ID and you inadvertently process a reportable payment.

I do this little trick to note who has a tax ID onFile, who does not.

**Agnetha Fältskog '   Vs   Jonhjuus Van Luarjwijck. **

So, in my AP-Universe, the one with the ' is one with <u>no</u> SSN on file (Agnetha), a reimbursement payee – no service payment until the dot (W-9 information) is added. While Johnjuus's records do include the tax ID (the dot indicates it), and also Johnjuus' account is set up for ACH. Of course, you can find all this information in the vendor records. But, often, often, you must be able to assess the situation so much quicker, or by looking at an issued check. My tricks-notes do work, trust me – and they don't hinder clearing of checks or deposit of the ACH.

In real life, reportable payments <u>are</u> made to payees with no W-9 on file. It just happens, sometimes. If all later attempts to collect the W-9 fail, you may still process a 1099 with no payee tax ID and *bite the bullet*, pay the IRS fee.

Any US business or person must be able to supply form W-9. *A foreign payee cannot sign form W-9* and the most recent version of form W-9 has an important clarification about the W-9 filing requirement asking to certify that the person or business, named on the W-9, is a "US citizen or other US person" and requiring a "Signature of US person". Further in the W-9 instructions you can find the following: "If you are a foreign person, do not use Form W-9".

Why can't a foreign person who possesses a valid US social security or other tax ID number sign the W-9? <u>Paying foreign payees requires a statutory 30% tax withholding</u>, unless one of the IRS tax exemption codes can be applied. Not determining a proper residency status may cause tax liability, which adds up close to half of the payment amount processed improperly under the US residency assumption. *Example:*

Payment of $100 was made, with an assumption of the US tax residency based on completed form W-9. 30% tax was not applied. Gross up the amount to what it should have been to issue a net $100 check after withholding 30% tax. $100 / 70% (100/0.7) = 143. <u>*Back-tax owed to the IRS is $43 plus fees and penalties.*</u>

Keep in mind that many times form W-9 is completed by foreign businesses or individuals that have valid US tax IDs, e.g. ITIN. This is improper unless you can establish that such businesses or individuals are US tax residents. The IRS and SSA rules are being tightened and no foreign individuals can obtain SSN now. Foreign individuals are issued Individual Taxpayer ID Numbers (ITIN) if there is a need. Any ITIN number is structured as 9xx-7x-xxxx or 9xx-8xx-xxxx. You should be able to recognize ITINs vs. SSNs.

How can a foreign individual get an SSN (vs. ITIN)? It is impossible these days, but it was possible before year 2003. All such SSN recipients who used to be temporary US visa visitors, if still in the US since 2003, are US tax residents at this time, so they can legally complete from W-9 for you.

For all domestic businesses and persons, form W-9 has two options for the name – *Name* (as shown on your income tax return) and *Business name* (that is, DBA – *Doing Business As*, not the tax name). This may be confusing for many; *Business name/DBA* may be the same as the *Tax Name*. But many a time *Business name/DBA* is not the *Tax Name* and since there is no associated tax ID for *Business name/DBA*, you may end up supplying technically incorrect information (if 1099 filing is required) to the IRS. The IRS will ask you to correct this discrepancy by mailing to you Notice CP-2100A (also called the B-Notice, but the two are different documents of the same process).

It is very important to understand, based on the completed form W-9, what form of business ownership the payee is formed under. The appropriate box must be checked. If the *Individual/sole proprietor or single-member LLC* box is checked, a person's name must appear in the *Name* box and a social security number provided (EIN for single-member LLC). For all other forms of business ownership, the *EIN* (employer identification number) must be provided. A *Limited Liability Company (LLC)* may be treated for tax purposes as a (1) *disregarded entity*, (2) *corporation* or (3) *partnership*. This is an important distinction to keep in mind since the corporate treatment does not require you to file form 1099. Corporate exemption does not apply to medical and legal LLCs and corporations.

Partnership form of business ownership <u>does</u> require the 1099 filing. This is a fine point to understand and apply. I believe that given the importance of practical

W-9/1099 corporation-partnership classification it is worth a more in- depth analysis. Nathan M. Bisk, JD, CPA provides an excellent description of this partnership-corporation selection in his books "CPA Review: Regulations":

Under the 'check-the-box' regulations, an eligible entity may elect its classification for federal tax purposes. An eligible entity is an entity that does not meet the definition of a corporation under the regulations, and is not a single owner entity, trust, or otherwise subject to special treatment under the IRC. If the entity fails to elect a classification, the regulations provide a default classification. The use is broader than the common law meaning and may include groups not commonly called partnerships. (a) A partnership is a syndicate, group, pool, joint venture, or other unincorporated entity through which a business is carried on, and which is not a corporation, trust, or estate. (b) Mere co-ownership of property is not a partnership. However, if the entity provides services in conjunction with the use of the property by the lessee or licensee, the entity may be characterized as a partnership. (c) Limited partnerships are subject to the same rules as general partnerships. (d) Limited liability entities may be classified for federal tax purposes as either corporations or partnerships. Limited liability companies (LLC), limited liability partnerships (LLP), professional limited liability companies, etc. are frequently designed to take advantage of the pass-through tax status of partnerships and limited legal liability of corporations, but the partnership tax status is not automatic. Unless a limited liability entity meets conditions that require it to be taxed as a corporation or it elects to be so treated, it is treated as a partnership for tax purposes.

Section 3 of the W-9 shows seven check boxes; just one must be checked. For a tax-exempt nonprofit corporation, check - Other, write – Tax Exempt 501-c-3 Corporation (or other IRS nonprofit or governmental code as applicable).

Governmental, not-for-profit, and other tax-exempt businesses and organizations must enter the *Exempt Payee Code* if one is available from the list of codes found in the instructions for form W-9 revised in October 2018. [Note that 501(c)(3) not-for-profit organizations fall within IRC Section 501(a), Exemption Payee "1", Exempt from FATCA "A".]

The following codes identify payees that are exempt from backup withholding: 1 - An organization exempt from tax under section 501(a), any IRA, or a custodial account under section 403(b)(7) if the account satisfies the requirements of section 401(f)(2). 2 - The United States or any of its agencies or instrumentalities. 3 - A state, the District of Columbia, a possession of the United States, or any of their political subdivisions or instrumentalities. 4 - A foreign government or any of its political subdivisions, agencies, or instrumentalities. 5 – A corporation. 6 – A dealer in securities or commodities required to register in the United States, the District of Columbia, or a possession of the United States. 7 - A futures commission merchant registered with the Commodity Futures Trading Commission. 8 - A real estate investment trust. 9 - An entity registered at all times during the tax year under the Investment Company Act of 1940. 10 - A common trust fund operated by a bank under section 584(a). 11 - A financial institution. 12 - A middleman known in the investment community as a nominee or custodian. 13 - A trust exempt from tax under section 664 or described in section 4947.

There are boxes on form W-9 for address, account number and signature. Having properly completed form W-9 on file fulfills your responsibility to collect payees' tax ID and business ownership status information. You may find it useful to register with *Dan & Bradstreet* services (http://www.dnb.com) to validate companies' names and receive other relevant for your accounts payable purposes information.

Another form required by your company (not the IRS) to be completed by all new payees should be your internally created *New Payee Questionnaire*. This form should have additional payee's information, such as contact names, phone numbers, fax numbers, email addresses, company website, remittance address(s), bank account information (ABA/routing number, account number, account name, accounts receivable contact information and email address). Bank account information may be provided on the payee's dedicated form and supported by a copy of vendor's check usually marked "void". The *New Payee Questionnaire* must require immigration status, tax residency and foreign business or individual's US tax ID information and certification, something that form W-9 is not designed to do.

Failure to furnish form W-9 to you must trigger back-up withholding at the rate of 24%. The back-up withholding is reported to the IRS on form *945* and to the payee on form 1099-MISC. I have not processed one such 24% withholding in my career, although had set up many payees for the back-up withholding. All payees will comply with the W-9 requirement once you explain what the noncompliance may trigger: back-up taxes and, possibly, IRS audit.

Remember that "no W-9 on file" is not a stalemate – take the tax and move on (by now you should be able to discern that this advice is more theoretical than practical).

Did I say that the foreign persons cannot by the IRS regulation sign form W-9? What form do the temporary residents sign to certify their possession of a US tax ID number? Many a time you hear the advice to "sign the appropriate form W-8". This is wrong. First, there may be no appropriate form for a temporary visitor to sign, and second, those forms W-8xxx (W-8BEN, W-8ECI, W-8EXP, W-8IMY) are not used for collection nonresident alien tax IDs. Those forms serve other purposes: W-8BEN to certify foreign status of beneficial owner for United States tax withholding, W-ECI to certify foreign person's claim that income is effectively connected with the conduct of a trade or business in the United States. The bottom line is that any form W-8xxx (W-8 has been out of use for more than ten years) cannot be used with the temporary residents instead of form W-9. Allowing the foreign persons to use forms W-8xxx may give them a false impression that they may be eligible to certain US tax benefits when, in fact, they are not. You can read more about forms W-8xxx on the following IRS webpage:

http://www.irs.gov/uac/Form-W-8,-Certificate-of-Foreign-Status

If you need to collect a US tax ID (ITIN) from a temporary US visitor, use your internally developed New Payee Questionnaire, on which you should also ask about the visa status and other nonresident alien-related questions (history of priory US visits, copies of various immigration forms (visa, I94, DS2019, I20, etc.).

The most recent updates to form W-9 were officiated in October 2018 to reflect the final amendment to the Income Tax Regulations commonly known as the Foreign Tax Compliance Act, or FATCA. The FATCA reporting requires a participating foreign financial institution to report all US account holders that are specified US persons. The FATCA is designed to better track worldwide income of US persons by requiring much greater information sharing by the US and foreign financial institutions. Certain payees are exempt from FATCA reporting. There is a list of codes (A through M) provided in the instructions to form W-9.

The new W-9 form has the former "Exempt Payee" section, which was used on all previous forms W-9 by not-for-profit organizations, United States agencies, etc., renamed "Exemptions" and separated into two sub-sections: the familiar "Exempt payee code" and the new *"Exemption from FATCA reporting code"*. The completion of the FATCA exemption code section does not affect your company's new payees or 1099 processing unless your company makes payments to financial institutions which are required to report income payments to account holders who are US persons under the FATCA regulations.

Request for Taxpayer
Identification Number and Certification

▶ Go to *www.irs.gov/FormW9* for instructions and the latest information.

Give Form to the
requester. Do not
send to the IRS.

1 Name (as shown on your income tax return). Name is required on this line; do not leave this line blank.

2 Business name/disregarded entity name, if different from above

3 Check appropriate box for federal tax classification of the person whose name is entered on line 1. Check only **one** of the following seven boxes.

☐ Individual/sole proprietor or single-member LLC ☐ C Corporation ☐ S Corporation ☐ Partnership ☐ Trust/estate

☐ Limited liability company. Enter the tax classification (C=C corporation, S=S corporation, P=Partnership) ▶ _____

Note: Check the appropriate box in the line above for the tax classification of the single-member owner. Do not check LLC if the LLC is classified as a single-member LLC that is disregarded from the owner unless the owner of the LLC is another LLC that is **not** disregarded from the owner for U.S. federal tax purposes. Otherwise, a single-member LLC that is disregarded from the owner should check the appropriate box for the tax classification of its owner.

☐ Other (see instructions) ▶

4 Exemptions (codes apply only to certain entities, not individuals; see instructions on page 3):

Exempt payee code (if any) _____

Exemption from FATCA reporting code (if any) _____

(Applies to accounts maintained outside the U.S.)

5 Address (number, street, and apt. or suite no.) See instructions.

6 City, state, and ZIP code

Requester's name and address (optional)

7 List account number(s) here (optional)

Part I Taxpayer Identification Number (TIN)

Enter your TIN in the appropriate box. The TIN provided must match the name given on line 1 to avoid backup withholding. For individuals, this is generally your social security number (SSN). However, for a resident alien, sole proprietor, or disregarded entity, see the instructions for Part I, later. For other entities, it is your employer identification number (EIN). If you do not have a number, see *How to get a TIN*, later.

Note: If the account is in more than one name, see the instructions for line 1. Also see *What Name and Number To Give the Requester* for guidelines on whose number to enter.

Social security number

☐☐☐ – ☐☐ – ☐☐☐☐

or

Employer identification number

☐☐ – ☐☐☐☐☐☐☐

Part II Certification

Under penalties of perjury, I certify that:

1. The number shown on this form is my correct taxpayer identification number (or I am waiting for a number to be issued to me); and
2. I am not subject to backup withholding because: (a) I am exempt from backup withholding, or (b) I have not been notified by the Internal Revenue Service (IRS) that I am subject to backup withholding as a result of a failure to report all interest or dividends, or (c) the IRS has notified me that I am no longer subject to backup withholding; and
3. I am a U.S. citizen or other U.S. person (defined below); and
4. The FATCA code(s) entered on this form (if any) indicating that I am exempt from FATCA reporting is correct.

Certification instructions. You must cross out item 2 above if you have been notified by the IRS that you are currently subject to backup withholding because you have failed to report all interest and dividends on your tax return. For real estate transactions, item 2 does not apply. For mortgage interest paid, acquisition or abandonment of secured property, cancellation of debt, contributions to an individual retirement arrangement (IRA), and generally, payments other than interest and dividends, you are not required to sign the certification, but you must provide your correct TIN. See the instructions for Part II, later.

Sign Here	Signature of U.S. person ▶	Date ▶

(Form W-9, revised in October 2018)

SSN's, ITIN's, EIN's, ATIN's and other numbers

When you receive information of a tax ID number on form W-9 you accept it *in good faith*. But, as an accounts payable professional, you know that all US tax ID numbers have nine digits. If there are less than nine, you should inquire further and not process the W-9 information. A social security number (*SSN*) is assigned by the Social Security Administration (SSA) to US persons and, prior to year 2002, was issued to foreign persons as well. (http://www.ssa.gov/online/ss-5.pdf).

Possession of a valid SSN does not indicate the US residency status of an individual.

ITIN is an individual taxpayer identification number; it is issued by the IRS upon completion of form *W7 - Application for Individual Taxpayer Identification Number (http://www.irs.gov/pub/irs-pdf/fw7.pdf)*. It is more proper for a foreign person to have the ITIN than the SSN. The ITIN always begins with number "9" and has numbers "7" or "8" in the fourth place. You are not required to know this or verify form W-9 or other tax ID source information based on this rule. But, if you spot possible errors, based on this information, and inquire further to correct the tax ID provided, you will improve the quality of your 1099 and 1042-S reporting and avoid possible IRS inquiry about wrong tax IDs later. Both SSN and ITIN are written in the 3-2-4 format (xxx-xx-xxxx). The IRS requires that you keep the correct format, SSN or EIN, when reporting to the agency.

While both SSN-ITIN-ATIN and EIN groups are unique nine-digit numbers, the IRS requires to 'make every effort to ensure that you have the correct type of number reported in the correct format'. An ATIN is an Adoption Taxpayer Identification Number issued by the Internal Revenue Service as a temporary taxpayer identification number for the child in a domestic adoption where the adopting taxpayers do not have and/or are unable to obtain the child's Social Security Number (SSN).

EIN stands for the Employer Identification Number. The EIN is issued by the IRS and is written in the 2-7 format (xx-xxxxxxx) (http://www.irs.gov/pub/irs-pdf/fss4.pdf). Here too, you must be experienced enough to notice that different states (or, rather, EIN-issuing offices, IRS campuses) have identical first two-digit numbers of the EINs. A deviation from the rule should not trigger further inquiry once a payee has properly completed and signed form W-9 but may call for your own action to verify correctness of the information.

The best process to verify US tax IDs is to register with the IRS for the online TIN Matching using the following web-address:

https://la1.www4.irs.gov/e-services/Registration/Reg_Online/Reg_RegisterUserForm

The online IRS TIN matching is an immensely useful tool for any accounts payable professional. There are just too many scenarios when you want to check the accuracy of the tax IDs on file. The service does not allow to find out what the tax ID for the name or the name for the tax ID is, but to verify the correctness of "tax ID / name" combination information that you have. Too many attempts to verify similar information will lock your user account and require phone call to the IRS or registering online to have account re-activated (you will need to wait for an IRS letter in the mail with a new activation code).

Once I had a case when a person, who was reported to me by the IRS on form CP-2100A as not having the correct tax name or ID, would provide the same name and tax ID again and again. I tried to validate it using the IRS TIN matching system but would always get the same erroneous results - *TIN and Name combination does not match IRS records*. I did not want to report a very significant current year's dollar amount paid to the individual again using the same tax ID, having been made aware of the past discrepancy. The current year's payments were made prior to my receipt of the CP-2100A notice, a tricky-sticky situation. I boldly requested to see the person's SSN card and lo and behold, his last name was a two-part last name and the person was only using the second part, thinking that the first part of the last name is the middle name. It looked like this – John Paul Jones, with the *Paul Jones* being the official last name, while the person always used Jones as the only last name (intentionally or not, at least with may organization). I had matched the first name and the two-part last name to the same SSN successfully using the IRS TIN matching system and was able to untangle the mystery having my access to the IRS's TIN matching tool.

Any foreign tax ID cannot be accepted or used (other than as reference) for your US operations and tax reporting. *There may be instances when you accept reportable to the IRS payees <u>with no US tax IDs</u> into your accounts payable system*. It is possible to pay a *foreign service* provider who came to the US, earned fees for services, and got paid while possessing no US tax ID. Such payment <u>must be</u> taxed at a 30% rate and reported to the IRS on form 1042-S with an affidavit that certifies your inability (understandingly so, as the payee does not have US tax ID number) to obtain a tax ID. The IRS will accept your reporting only when you support it by the withheld (or grossed-up) and remitted taxes; otherwise (without taxes applied) it will highlight your non-compliance and assess past due taxes, fees and penalties.

Most of today's accounts payable systems validate tax numbers' 9-digits format, but not any other rules and standards built into the SSN's, ITIN's and EIN's structure. You can perform the analytical test yourself, based on the publicly available information. Social Security numbers is structured as follows:

i. *The first three digits indicate the State where Social Security number was issued.*
ii. *The middle two digits approximate year when SSN was issued. "00" was never used.*
iii. *The last four digits is a sequential number.*

The following are the first three-digit ranges assigned by state where SSN was issued:

001-003...	**New Hampshire**
004-007...	**Maine**
008-009...	**Vermont**
010-034...	**Massachusetts**
035-039...	**Rhode Island**
040-049...	**Connecticut**
050-134...	**New York**
135-158...	**New Jersey**

159-211...	Pennsylvania
212-220...	Maryland
221-222...	Delaware
223-231...	Virginia & West Virginia
232-232...	North Carolina
233-236...	Foreign nationals
237-246...	North Carolina
247-251...	South Carolina
252-260...	Georgia
267-267...	Florida
268-302...	Ohio
303-317...	Indiana
318-361...	Illinois
362-386...	Michigan
387-399...	Wisconsin
400-407...	Kentucky
408-415...	Tennessee
416-424...	Alabama
425-428...	Mississippi
429-432...	Arkansas
433-439...	Louisiana
440-448...	Oklahoma
449-467...	Texas
468-477...	Minnesota
478-485...	Iowa
486-500...	Missouri
501-502...	North Dakota
503-504...	South Dakota
505-508...	Nebraska
509-515...	Kansas
516-517...	Montana
518-519...	Idaho
520-520...	Wyoming
521-524...	Colorado
525-525...	New Mexico
526-527...	Arizona

528-529...	Utah
530-530...	Nevada
531-539...	Washington
540-544...	Oregon
545-573...	California
574-574...	Alaska
575-576...	Hawaii
577-579...	Washington, D.C.
580-584...	Puerto Rico & Virgin Islands
585-585...	New Mexico
586-586...	Guam, Samoa & Pacific Territories
587-588...	Mississippi
589-595...	Florida
596-599...	Foreign nationals
600-601...	Arizona
602-626...	California
627-699...	Foreign nationals
700-728...	R-type Retirement
729-999...	Other purposes

Individual Taxpayer ID Numbers, ITIN's (issued by the IRS) have the following format, no matter where or when they were issued:

9xx-7x-xxxx

9xx-8x-xxxx

An Adoption Taxpayer Identification Number (ATIN) is a temporary nine-digit number issued by the IRS to individuals who are in the process of legally adopting a U.S. citizen or resident child but who cannot get an SSN for that child in time to file their tax return.

It is also possible to better understand the EIN structure. Prefix 13 is issued for New York State businesses, 36 – Illinois. Read the below IRS information about the EIN prefixes. Your analysis for a Houston, TX business EIN may be as the following: 53-xxxxxxx, EIN with prefix 53 is issued in Austin, TX – the EIN appears to be correct. (Use the TIN matching system to do a full confirmation.)

(source: https://www.irs.gov/businesses/small-businesses-self-employed/how-eins-are-assigned-and-valid-ein-prefixes)

Prior to 2001, the first two digits of an EIN (the EIN Prefix) indicated the business was in a particular geographic area. In 2001, EIN assignment was centralized, although all 10 campuses can assign an EIN, if necessary.

As a result of the centralization effort, the EIN prefix no longer has the same significance. The EIN prefix now only indicates which campus assigned the EIN. Each campus has certain prefixes available for use, as well as prefixes that are solely for use by the online application and the Small Business Administration. The prefix breakdown is shown in the table below:

Campus/Other Location	Valid EIN Prefixes
Andover	*10, 12*

Campus/Other Location	Valid EIN Prefixes
Atlanta	60, 67
Austin	50, 53
Brookhaven	01, 02, 03, 04, 05, 06, 11, 13, 14, 16, 21, 22, 23, 25, 34, 51, 52, 54, 55, 56, 57, 58, 59, 65
Cincinnati	30, 32, 35, 36, 37, 38, 61
Fresno	15, 24
Kansas City	40, 44
Memphis	94, 95
Ogden	80, 90

Campus/Other Location	Valid EIN Prefixes
Philadelphia	33, 39, 41, 42, 43, 46, 48, 62, 63, 64, 66, 68, 71, 72, 73, 74, 75, 76, 77, 82, 83, 84, 85, 86, 87, 88, 91, 92, 93, 98, 99
Internet	20, 26, 27, 45, 46, 47, 81, 82
Small Business Administration (SBA)	31

New payee set up

Have your 1099 processing written up in policies and procedures. The 1099 policies and procedures must be approved and updated every time the process changes or once a year. The policies must describe your tax treatment and coding of the AP payments. The procedures describe how your department is processing the 1099's. The 1099 processing includes your AP activities that begin with collecting of form W-9, setting up new payee ID correctly with the proper 1099 "flags", processing invoices and payment requests of your payees. Every action of the 1099 process must be outlined in your policies and procedures for you to refer to, for others who will one day replace you, or as a basis and justifications of the actions that you take in relation to the 1099 processing.

When form W-9 is submitted by a payee, your next step is creating a payee ID, which is the next crucial step in the 1099 compliance process. To create a new payee, you need to submit *New Payee Setup* requisition form to a person who, according to the segregation of duties concept, has no other accounts payable function, but new payees' creation. You must have an established payee IDs creating system which is logical, understood, and consistent. I believe that using letters and numbers combination is the best system to unitize, where technically feasible. Using letters gives you more room to create new payees in the years to come, since there are 26 letters and (only) 10 numbers (0 to 9) to use in each place. There may be sequential "numbers only" payees IDs system, it assigns the next sequential number to each new payee. A six-digit payee ID format will allow for 1M less 1, i.e. 999,999 vendor IDs to create; think if this will be enough. Often a sequential vendor ID number if pre-fixed with V- (vs. C- for customers, E- for employees).

With the alpha-numerical manual vendors/payees ID system, I advise to use letters in the first eight places and digits in the remaining two. Following is an example of alpha-numerical system:

Payee name: **Fist American Brewing Company, Inc.**
Payee ID: **FIRSTAME01**

Payee name: **First American Consulting, LLC**
Payee ID: **FIRSTAME02**

You may find it a good practice to eliminate the connecting conjunction "and" (or "&") from the payee ID structure:

Payee name: **Levi & Strook, LP**
Payee ID: **LEVISTRO01**

There may be certain 1099 reports, depending on the system that your company is using, where only vendor IDs are showing against other AP data. It is impossible, using the "numbers only" payee IDs, to have a quick understanding of the payees' names without translating the payees' IDs into the names first. It does save time during AP data entry as well, to understand which payee is being processed by just seeing payee's ID.

A system for coding individuals' names may be as following: use last name in places 1-7, first initial in place

8, sequential digits in places 9-10. Use X's for short names or complete all eight available for name spots:

Payee Name: **Denny Laine**
Payee ID: **LAINEDXX01** or **LAINEDEN01**

Shorten the lust name if longer than 7 characters:

Payee Name: **Zebulon Jefferson**
Payee ID: **JEFFERSZ01**

Never allow for space(s) in the payee IDs:

Payee name: **Pete Towns Hend**
Vendor ID: **TOWNSHEP01**

If the business name is different from the legal name, use the name under which the business normally operates, shows on the invoice, and represents itself under. Add a different tax name, if necessary, in the *Legal Name or 1099 Name* field in the payee set up. The legal name may be very unfamiliar to people involved in the accounts payable process – making the legal name main search criteria may delay the search process or, worse, lead to an assumption that payee is a new payee, which results in (attempt of) duplicate payee creation. Duplicate payee's creation is one of the big *No-no's* in the accounts payable. One way to avoid this is to run duplicate payees' tax ID report or "flag and stop" new payee tax IDs entry (upon new payee creation) as a duplication of the existing one.

A payee may have different "remit-to" addresses. Usually, these multiple-remittance addresses payees are large corporations, such as AT&T, Verizon, or various IRS's processing centers. Large companies process different locations' invoice at their different offices around the US.

What is more critical is to realize, in some cases, that "a new remittance address" for identically sounding business name is not a new remittance address at all, but a remittance address for a different business altogether, possibly a *franchise* which operates under the same brand name, but a different tax name and tax ID. Franchise is a right to operation under a well-known business name, such as McDonald's True Value Hardware, with each franchisee being a separate business for all other purposes: "*McDonald's continues to be recognized as a premier franchising company around the world. More than 80% of our restaurants worldwide are owned and operated by our Franchisees*" (quoted from the McDonald Co. website, below):

http://www.aboutmcdonalds.com/mcd/franchising.html

Again, form W-9 provides the information about all the critical data in this less than clear situation, such as Business Name and tax ID number.

The default remittance address should be the most used remittance address. Any remittance address that is no longer used should be inactivated, but not deleted or overwritten with a new address, to preserve the historic records in the accounts payable system. Make sure to update your "1099 address" with an updated remittance or corporate headquarters address.

I already mention my 'tricks' that allow me to access vendor status looking at the name alone: **Bob Ng.** \ -

name set up tells me that Bob's account has W-9 (dot) and ACH bank information processed (backslash). Again, neither dot nor backslash hinder check or ACH bank processing.

Depending on the complexity and payment volumes of your accounts payable operation there may be more, or fewer people involved in the AP review and data entry process. When an invoice is approved by a buying department, it is routed to accounts payable administrator who reviews it, assigns payee ID, codes it (indicates 1099 code (if applies), cost center ID, account number, etc.), type of payment (if both checks and EFT's are processed to pay a vendor), reviews any adjustments made to the original invoice, possibly completes data entry sheet and sends it to the accounts payable data entry clerk. A 1099-flagged payment voucher must create form 1099 even for a vendor which is not coded for 1099 reporting (e.g. a service payment made to a person who later became your company's W-2 employee). Web-based ERP workflow systems follow the same purchasing format: Purchase Request – PO – Receipt – Invoice – AP reviews/approvals – Payment Processing.

Entered into the AP system invoice gets assigned a system payment number (transaction number, payment voucher number). The number will come in handy in future 1099 reviews and reports. All entered invoices are sent to the person(s) who does the pre- or post-printing payments verification. I had switched my AP department to conducting the final payment review before posting/paying open payment vouchers during the times of the EFT/ACHs transitioning from paper checks.

The ERP systems are here to eliminate all other types of legacy accounting applications for all businesses, large or small. The AP data entry activities performed in the accounts payable department are reduced when using the ERP, since invoices are sent as data feeds by those of your vendors which are technically equipped to do it, or entered remotely by users in different offices, cost centers, colleges, or other reporting units. Departmental approval is performed first, and then approved invoices appear in the accounts payable administrators' system (the audit trail marks every processing step generated by the ERP).

Usually, there is a three-step review and approval process of all e-invoices in the ERPs AP workflow (besides the data entry): departmental (including the 1099 coding), accounts payables and final review before payments are paid and released. There may be added processing layers in cases when payments exceed certain dollar thresholds (senior management review), payments made to nonresident aliens (nonresident alien tax compliance manager's review) or capital assets purchases (general accounting manager's review).

All ERP systems have payment documentation imaged and attached to the respective AP records – it is available for immediate 1099 review, based on relevant reference criteria: payment number, payment voucher number or invoice number. Imaging of payment documents used with the legacy AP systems is one huge benefit the accounts payment departments are reaping since early 2000's. I cannot praise the imaging functionality more than I have been doing since I started having access to it before my switching to the ERP system use. All older AP systems can be equipped with a separate payment documents imaging system, which must be updated with all newly processed payment documents; scanned after processing and indexed to allow for search based on payment or invoice number.

You will immediately realize how outdated and cumbersome the 1099 paper processing is, once you get the taste of having the AP documentation digitized and available on your computer screen. Also, there is no greater embarrassment for the Accounts Payable department than losing a (not yet scanned and indexed) paper payment request and not being able to release a processed payment or retrieve an AP document because of that.

New payees' initial setup information and supporting documents (form W-9, New Payee Questionnaire) must be imaged and accessible from the *Payee* general informational menu for future 1099 references and verifications.

Independent Contractor: How, When & Where

One of the most important 1099-related determinations that is made in the Accounts Payable is the proper classification of the independent contractors and coding all such payee accordingly for 1099 reporting. Who is considered an independent contractor? Can one choose to be an independent contractor if it is more beneficial for the individual's tax purposes rather than becoming a company's employee? ***Who is an employee and who is an independent contractor?*** The following is the IRS's approach to this crucial determination, which is made in the Accounts Payable department and cannot be decided by any other than the IRS mandated method:

The general rule is that an individual is an independent contractor if the payer has the right to control or direct only the result of the work and not what will be done and how it will be done. The earnings of a person who is working as an independent contractor are subject to Self-Employment Tax.

It is critical that business owners correctly determine whether the individuals providing services are employees or independent contractors. Generally, you must withhold income taxes, withhold, and pay Social Security and Medicare taxes, and pay unemployment tax on wages paid to an employee. You do not generally have to withhold or pay any taxes on payments to independent contractors.

(http://www.irs.gov/Businesses/Small-Businesses-&-Self-Employed/Independent-Contractor-(Self-Employed)-or-Employee%3F)

An independent contractor is an individual or business providing services free from direction and control of performance including the means and methods used. Independent contractors fall into two categories: a company or firm providing service or individuals who are clearly in business for themselves such as doctors, computer programmers, accountants, lawyers, construction contractors, electricians, and other. It is the responsibility of the department that hires independent contractors to make *initial* determination as to whether to classify an individual as an employee or an independent contractor.

The IRS has issued general guidelines rather than more specific regulations on the employee vs. independent contractor distinction. Each contract with independent contractor must be evaluated very carefully. There is no single criterion which determines classification one way or another. Extra caution must be taken before signing contracts with individuals (1) not ordinarily in consulting business or (2) with past company's employees.

The general IRS rule is: if an individual is subject to the control or direction of another merely as to the <u>result</u> to be accomplished by the work and not as to the means and methods for accomplishing the results, such individual is an independent contractor, rather than an employee. Most of the IRS's criteria for determining the status of a service provider hinge on the idea of *the degree of control the employer exercises over the individual*. Keep in mind that for the IRS, it does not matter whether this control is actually exercised, just that a relationship of control exists. In each case, it is very important to consider all the facts - no single fact provides the answer.

The IRS developed a *20-Factor Test* to determine whether a business controls and directs a service provider or has a right to do so. The factors (questions), applied to each individual circumstance under which services are to be performed, determine the individual's classification. The questions must be objectively and consistently applied to determine the individual's correct status. To be classified as independent contractor, answers to question 1 and question 2 must be "No". If the predominance of answers to the remaining 18 questions is "No", the individual is an independent contractor. If answers to question 1 and question 2 are "Yes", the individual is an employee; otherwise, predominance of "Yes" answers for the remaining 18 questions is indicative of the individual's employee status.

The 20 questions are:

1. **Is the individual directed by someone in the company where and how the work is to be done?**
2. **Is the company providing detailed instructions or training to enable the individual to perform the work in a particular timeframe or manner?**
3. **Can the individual perform the work without any risk of direct economic loss to himself/herself?**
4. **Are the services provided by the individual an integral part of company's operations?**
5. **Must the services be performed specifically by the individual (rather than by someone else employed by the individual)?**

6. Will the company hire, supervise, or pay others to help the individual on the job?

7. Is there a continuing work relationship between the individual and the company?

8. Is the work schedule set by someone at the company?

9. Is the individual required to devote his/her full-time work to the company?

10. Is the work required to be performed on the company's premises, or in specific places designated by the company?

11. Is the sequence of work set by someone at the company?

12. Are regular oral or written reports required to be submitted to the company by the individual?

13. Is the method of payment based on hourly, weekly, or monthly fees (as opposed to commission or by the project/job)?

14. Are business and/or travel expenses reimbursed?

15. Does the company furnish the tools, equipment and materials used by the individual?

16. Can the individual perform the work without making or having made any investment in equipment or offices?

17. Does the individual perform services exclusively for the company rather than working for many companies at the same time?

18. Does the individual make his/her services regularly available to other businesses?
19. Is the individual subject to dismissal for reasons other than nonperformance of contract specifications?
20. Can the individual end his/her working relationship with the company at any time without incurring liability for failure to complete the job?

Answering just the first two questions of the test provides quick answer to the employee or independent contractor determination based on the basic test: whether a business directs or has right to direct a worker as to *how*, *when* and *where* the work should be done.

Moving Expenses and 1099 Reporting

Form 1099 is not used to report qualified moving expenses reimbursements.

Qualified Moving Expenses Reimbursements No Longer Excluded from Employees' Income, with Two Exceptions

For 2018 through 2025, employers must include moving expense reimbursements in employees' wages. The new tax law suspends the exclusion for qualified moving expense reimbursements.

Exception 1: Members of the U.S. Armed Forces can still exclude qualified moving expense reimbursements from their income if:

- They are on active duty
- They move pursuant to a military order and incident to a permanent change of station
- The move expenses would qualify as a deduction if the employee did not get a reimbursement

Exception 2: Employers may exclude from wages any 2018 reimbursements to or payments on behalf of employees for moving expenses incurred for a move that took place prior to January 1, 2018, and which would have been deductible had they been paid prior to that date. See Notice 2018-75

Processing forms 1099 and 1096

What is the busiest period in the Accounts Payable department? Without a doubt, it is the months of January through mid-April every year. This is the time when forms 1099s and 1042-S are processed by the AP departments and forms 1040 are filed by the payees with the IRS. While it may depend on the types of payees and payments that your accounts payable department processed during the previous year, the 1099 review still presents a challenge to meet right after the New Year holidays. I have never experienced an easy "push of a button" kind of 1099 processing. I can imagine that the 1099 processing is probably fully automated in a bank processing forms 1099-INT (interest payments of $10 and more) where all the information for the amounts paid and recipients of interest is in the bank's AP system – this is a straight-forward process. I can guess that your department's payees and payment types are much more diverse than interest recipients of a commercials bank. Correct processing of forms 1099 is a time consuming and tedious task for most of medium to large businesses.

An orderly and controlled 1099 process begins with a proper new payee set up in the AP system. This is the time to ensure that there will be less hassle down the road. Collect properly completed forms W-9 for all new vendors with no exception. Pay attention to the DBA (Doing Business As) name and the legal name. Tax ID numbers are assigned to legal names and not DBA names. Having DBA names on forms 1099 triggers a voluminous B-notice letter from the IRS.

Reading and understanding form W-9 and transferring the W-9 information into accounts payable system must be done by a trained person, who comprehends well the concepts of legal name, DBA, and related tax ID rules, forms of business ownership and rules of the US tax IDs structure. If a business name has the *LLC* at the end, form W-9 must state how the LLC (Limited Liability Company) is treated for tax purposes - as 'disregarded entity', corporation or partnership. If there is a person's name in the "name, as shown on your income tax return" field and no social security number provided (but the employer ID) – ask for clarifications (individual's name, being the legal name, requires social security number to be provided, not employer identification number, unless incorporated under the individual's name). I want to emphasize – **an efficient and quality 1099 year-end processing never ends – tend to it all times by maintaining the integrity of the accounts payable system payees' records.** New form W-9, revised by the IRS in October 2018, requires FATCA related codes entered in the 'exempt' section of the W-9. By the way, the 'not-for-profit' coding is '1' and 'A' for most 501(c) (3) companies.

Start your 1099 review on December 1st for the preceding eleven months of the year. Complete the 11/12 or the review job in December and review the month of December in January. This will leave plenty of time in January to better review and structure the process and not be pressed too much by the January 31st deadline - now, the IRS reporting deadline as well, for Nonemployee compensation, Box 7.

Another important consideration for starting it all in December; if there are any AP and payroll unjustifiable overlaps, they should be 'moved' to payroll and W2 forms. The best time to do it is before the year end in December.

The Transmitter Control Code (TCC) is required to be able to submit the 1099 to the IRS electronically. Read *IRS Publication 1220* to learn how to apply for the transmitter control code (TCC) and process forms 1099 online. The extra month (March) before your 1099 electronic reporting is due to the IRS allows extra time to correct any discrepancy reported to you by the 1099 recipients.   Any 1099 corrections done before submitting files to the IRS is a much easier process, since correcting 1099's after the IRS reporting requires correcting of both *Copy B* (for recipient) and *copy A* (for the IRS) along with form 1096, which (1099 copy A and form 1096) are then mailed to the IRS.

The correction process brings about another issue – mailing addresses on forms 1099. A verification process must be in place to assures that all forms 1099 are mailed to the most recent and valid addresses. Base this review on the last remittance address used to mail payments to. With the EFT's payment method becoming more and more dominant, it is possible to have old physical address information on file, while maintaining correct banking information. Therefore, pay attention to all returned to you by the USPS forms 1099 and re-address them promptly.

All 1099 recipients should duly receive the 1099 forms not only to allow them a timely tax reporting, but to give them an opportunity to provide feedback on any possible errors or discrepancies on forms 1099 that you have mailed out. It is a very difficult situation to find yourself in when a misaddressed form is lost in transit, the intended recipient does not include the 1099 income on the tax return and is later contacted by the IRS about the under-reported income, resulting in additional taxes, penalties, and fees. To make the matter worse, the information on lost forms 1099 may be incorrect as reported to the IRS.

The order and ease of the 1099 review depends on quality of your accounts payable processing during the previous year. I admit that with large-scale distributed AP operations you cannot always control the AP quality 100%; you cannot review all payments processed during the year, cannot review correctness of payments coding.

The accounts payable data entry may be also partially outsourced to remote offices and locations while the central-office Accounts Payable department only reviews the AP data entry but does not originate them. There is a higher probability of the AP tax reporting input errors in larger Accounts Payable departments, with high volume payment activity, numerous payment types made, and constant pressure to keep the AP payments processing flow. Even with the best internal controls and policies and procedures it is possible to have errors in the AP system that generates the 1099 data.

The quantity of errors is also affected by the AP system in use; the ERP's capturing all information and having more built-in intelligence is far superior to the "fractured databases" scenario with independent processing systems used for various business purposes (AP, payroll, nonresident alien, imaging databases). Example: *A payment was made to a nonresident alien in the US and reported on form 1042-S, but during the last year the person became US permanent resident and now his service payments are reported on form 1099. Unless the information was transferred from the nonresident alien database to the AP database, the change in status will not be reflected automatically in the AP database.*

There are many other 1099 pitfalls that one may get into – let's review one more:

An independent contractor, who had received reportable service payments in the prior to the reporting year, visited your company last year and only asked to be reimbursed for travel. A 1099 form was issued with the travel reimbursement payment amount on it, based on previous tax reporting classification.

There may be reimbursements to your company's employees for service payments to third parties; this should not be allowed by your reimbursement guidelines and all such service payments should be made directly to the service providers who are required to furnish forms W-9 and be set up properly as separate payees.

I recall a few instances when payments were requested to be made to individuals, but the 1099 tax names were corporate and non-reportable, *Inc.*-type names. This is incorrect and the trace of it goes back to receiving, reading, understanding, and entering the W-9 information properly into AP system.

<u>A payment should never be made to an individual who has a W-9 form submitted for a non-reportable, corporate-type business</u> (e.g. payments made to *Barry Miles*, while the W-9 (non-medical/legal service type) name on file is *B Miles Inc.*).

When I think and write about how *things should be* in the accounts payable department, I wonder how errors can ever sneak into the accounts payable process undetected. But you and I know that in the real world the imperfections do happen in the department's work for a variety of objective, subjective, staff-related, mood-related, valid, silly, and other reasons. *Set la vie,* but you cannot allow to have the same error happen again.

Remember that your company's employees must not be paid any kind of 1099-reportable compensation. All services performed by your company's employees must be processed through the Payroll Department. Ideally, even the out-of-pocket and travel reimbursements should be included with payroll payments. Processing a service payment from the Accounts Payable will result first in issuing of a 1099 form and subsequent voiding of the 1099 form and adjusting of the employee's W-2 form (W-2C). This will trigger your company's additional FICA and unemployment taxes liability and correction of the W-2 information already processed with the IRS; this is a very undesirable situation that can also invite an unwanted IRS's attention to your processing. Processing of form 1099 and W-2 for the same individual for the same year is possible when the individual initially was an independent contractor and later became employed by the company.

There are exceptions. One classical example of someone justifiably receiving both forms W2 and 1099 from the same business for the same period is often provided during the 1099 trainings seminars: Rocket Scientist cleans company's restrooms at nighttime. He is employed as a Rocket Scientist (W-2) and also contracted for independently servicing the company premises as a janitor, providing different kinds of services, and thus correctly receiving both forms 1099 and W-2. You will not see this in your practice.

Another 'suspect' W2 and 1099 recipient situation may come about when a former employee now provides independent consultant's 1099 services for the same business. The tax authorities may reasonably infer an illegal tax 'optimization' scheme in the same employment circumstances. It is a prudent and desired goal of the Accounts Payable department (in team with the payroll) to avoid overlapping of names on forms W2 and 1099. It is best to have both Accounts Payable and Payroll records within one system to assure a better and system-based checking on any employee payment processed through the accounts payable process vs. payroll records. A good practice is to include any proper AP payments to employees (such as travel, out of pocket, tuition reimbursements) with employees' payroll payments or via Concur or similar reimbursement systems.

One recent development in the Accounts Payable process, imaging of documents, made the 1099 review much more effective and efficient. Documents' images are now available within an ERP system or in a separate imaging module added to a legacy accounting system. AP documents may be submitted or uploaded for payment in the electronic format or paper received documents scanned and indexed before payments processing. This immediate access to the source payment documentation is a huge help during the 1099 review.

Every Accounts Payable department must have all processed payments in the electronic format - indexed and readily available for review.

Requesting paper documents for review from your in-house storage or, worse, outside storage location, waiting for documents to be delivered to your desk, is long and frustrating. Costs savings related to elimination of paper storage and document retrieval will quickly offset your investment in imaging systems and greatly improve the quality of your accounts payable work, not only your 1099 review.

90% of accounts payable 1099 process deals with generating forms 1099-NEC and 1099-MISC; the forms report payments (total payments made in a calendar year) of $600 and more made to non-corporate businesses (exclude limited liability companies (LLC) treated as corporations for tax purposes) for rents, services (including parts and materials), prizes and awards, other income payments, medical and healthcare payments and royalties of $10 and more. The exemption from reporting payments made to corporations does not apply to payments for legal and medical/health care payments to corporations. Do not report on forms 1099 wages paid to employees, payments for merchandise, telephone, freight, storage, or payment to tax-exempt organization.

Another unique reporting item on form 1099-MISC is the deceased employee's wages gross amount. You must report the accrued wages and other compensation paid after the date of death to the estate of beneficiary (in box 3). Note that in the year of death, when the social security taxes are withheld from the deceased wages, the income is reported on both forms W-9 and 1099-MISC.

General information can be found in the instructions for processing Form 1099-MISC on the following website:

http://www.irs.gov/uac/Form-1099-MISC,-Miscellaneous-Income-

The AP department may also process forms 1099-, 1099-INT, 1099-B and 1099-C. Refer to the following IRS website for more information on other forms 1099:

http://apps.irs.gov/app/picklist/list/formsInstructions.html?value=1099&criteria=formNumber

The accounts payable system must have the capability to "flag" reportable payees and assign 1099 income codes – rents, royalties, other income, medical and health care payments, nonemployee compensation. The 1099 "flag" may also be added during data entry of payments for both 1099 and non-1099 flagged payees.

Take time during the months of December and January – do not rush the 1099 review unless the last year's AP payments were straight-forward one type of payment (e.g. interest on deposits reported by bank), or low volume AP payments, which allow a quick 1099 review. When you believe that your 1099 file has tax IDs for all generated forms 1099 which are nine digits in length, in proper xxx-xx-xxxx (SSN/ITIN/ATIN) or xx-xxxxxxx (EIN) format (b) correct business names for the respective tax IDs (c) correct reported amounts (d) in correct income types boxes selected, and, finally (e) correct mailing address, you can print and mail 1099's out to recipients (post-marked no later than January 31st). By the way, the IRS, while requiring a correct format for the SSNs and EINs, accepts a tax number provided as one nine-digit number. But for your processing purposes it is better to differentiate between the SSN and EIN structure to better monitor the tax ID relation to the tax name.

I already mentioned the transmitter control code (TCC) you need to use the FIRE system. The online 1099 submission is a far superior process to the archaic filing of paper forms with the IRS. It allows for one extra month for review and corrections of forms 1099 (paper – due February 28, e-filing – March 31; only for other than Box 7 data), savings on cost of paper forms, printing and postage.

The FIRE System new account set up is found at this web-address:
https://fire.irs.gov/firev1r/Register.aspx

You must upload the 1099 text data file to the IRS website, or have your contracted third-party processor do it. If not formatted properly (the file should be a plain text file) the 1099 file will have "BAD" status. All *bad* files must be corrected through the 'Replace' process. The old bad file's result status will change to 'replaced' and a new corrected file submission will have 'GOOD, Not Released' status assigned to it. It will remain in this status for ten days after which the IRS will have the file accepted. Keep in mind, that during the ten days while the file is in 'Good, Not Released' status, you can call the IRS to have its processing stopped. The IRS will advise you to wait until the 'Good, Not Released' status changes to 'BAD', after which you can process another file using the 'replace' process.

All corrections of forms 1099 after filing them with the IRS are done on paper or online through the fire.irs.gov site; corrected paper forms 1099-MISC or 1099-NEC must be accompanied by summary form 1096. It is very important, while correcting forms 1099's based on the recipients' feedback and before reporting 1099 data to the IRS, to correct both *Copy B* (for recipient) and your 1099 IRS data file, which is later transmitted to the IRS. You do not want to have any discrepancy between what is reported to the recipients and the IRS – this is a very important consideration to keep in mind.

If any of your 1099-MISC or 1099-NEC forms are missing TINs (SSN or EIN) or have incorrect TINs, then the IRS will fine you $250 per form. If you file a correction within 30 days of the deadline, that fine can be reduced to $50. The penalty may be waived by showing the failure(s) was due to reasonable cause and not to willful neglect. What constitutes a reasonable cause?

Filers must establish that they acted in a responsible manner both before and after the failure occurred, and that: (1) There were significant mitigating factors (for example, an established history of filing information returns with correct TINs), (2) The failure was due to events beyond the filer's control (for example, a payee did not provide a correct name/TIN in response to a request for the corrected information). Acting in a responsible manner includes making an initial solicitation (request) for the payee's name and TIN and, if required, an annual solicitation. Upon receipt of this information, it must be used on any future information returns filed.

My last *1099 advice* is rather unusual. Being an accounts payable manager with many other responsibilities that fill my busy day in the office, I still stuff all processed forms 1099's in the envelopes *myself.* This tedious procedure allows for one last looks at each processed form, now printed on paper; it is a very laborious process, but I do it nonetheless and always find few issues during this process. I am very meticulous and patient, and not bossy – I stuff the 1099 envelopes myself. (In 2021 I had my www.1099tax.com mail the forms to the recipients for me – will continue this ⍰

The 1099 review is a time-consuming project for which there is no easy "system" solution. I was reassured early in year 2020 that this last manual 1099 review does make sense. When processing year 2019 forms 1099, I have noticed during my mailing of the forms that some amounts on the forms are incorrect, being much larger than what I ballpark-remembered they should be. I was baffled to say the least; this has happened after a thorough review of the 1099 forms and necessary adjustments to them – the 1099 forms were supposed to be flawless. It later transpired, after my emergency investigation of the situation, that my company's new ERP system was doubling the reported amounts for payees who received wire transfers (Fedwires) 1099 reportable payments every time I updated the 1099 totals during the review and correction process. The reason is still being investigated, but the damage could have been done if I had trusted the systems blindly and was not a quality freak.

Another check point for this situation is of course a comparison of the '1099 boxes totals' of the manual file to the system records; that, again, is possible if one keeps a tally of the 1099 amounts in a separate file and doesn't rely on the system alone to keep accurate records.

Here is one more practical advice: err on the side of over-reporting and not the other way around. *A Big Corporation* that sells you "merchandise" and receives form 1099 from you will not even bother to call to have the 1099 cancelled. However, an individual who finds discrepancy on form 1099 will contact you (remember to use the most current and verified address). You do not want the IRS auditors to find reportable payments processed by your Accounts Payable department and not reported. Remember, *when in doubt – mail it out –* well, yes, in this situation, do.

Correct and reissue the 1099 forms based on the 1099 recipients' feedback and adjust the IRS data file accordingly. Re-mail promptly all returned by the USPS (as undeliverable) forms 1099 to corrected addresses – leave no form returned and not re-mailed.

The 1099 reporting process is often an adversarial process that receives little appreciation by the recipients or your company's top managers; the reporting informs many recipients of additional tax liability and your company management may be contacted by complaining 1099 recipients who didn't receive relief from the tax reporting after their initial contacting and pleading with you. Many individuals are under the impression, falsely given to them by the departments and branches that initiated the contracts, that the payments made will not be reportable and reported to the recipients. This is especially true for companies that make a variety of diverse payments. Processing of 1099 often requires a degree of personal and professional character fortitude, thorough understanding of the process and knowing that your actions contribute to a better compliance and fiscal health of your company.

During the reporting period, besieged by the 1099 recipients who provide all kinds of reasons why the 1099 reporting must be reversed, quoting the IRS regulations, reminding of verbal promises of non-reporting made to them, or their tax accountants sending technical 'tricks' to zero the reported amounts, I often jokingly say to myself: *The Pledge of Allegiance in the morning, a pint of beer at night – it'll be alright.*

Commercial cards' 1099 reporting: The IRS's section 6050W requires merchant banks to report to the IRS 1099 data processed through their networks. It is no longer your department's responsibility to issue forms 1099 for reportable payments made with commercial credit cards. The 6050W regulation came as great relief to the AP world; it was very difficult to properly report on commercial cards merchants over which accounts payable departments had no processing controls:

Payments made with a credit card or payment card and certain other types of payments, including third party network transactions, must be reported on Form 1099-MISC by the payment settlement entity under section

6050W and are not subject to reporting on Form 1099-MISC. (1099 IRS Instructions)

IRS Notice CP-2100A and Backup Withholding

We are notifying you that payee information may be incorrect. You may need to begin backup withholding. This is the beginning of Notice CP-2100A. The language "may be incorrect" means that the **tax IDs** information or, note this, **tax names,** as provided on forms 1099-MISC, which you had filed earlier in the year, are incorrect. Some tax IDs and tax names do not match the IRS records. It is important to understand that notice CP-2100A does not tell you to assume (although it may be the case) that listed on the notice tax IDs are incorrect. It tells you that the IRS could not match the reported tax IDs with the reported tax names on your submitted forms 1099 and, as a result, could not track and compare reported by you (on from 1099) income to the income reported by the individuals and businesses who received your forms 1099. Therefore, your will be looking for errors in two places: tax IDs and/or respective tax names.

Why should I be analyzing this topic and not simply request a new form W-9 completed from all listed on the notice CP-2100A payees? For two reasons, after reviewing the documents on file you may realize that some tax IDs or tax ID-associated names are not those reported to you by the payee on form W-9s. It was your internal clerical error and must be resolved internally. It can be fixed on the spot.

If the IRS reports to you as incorrect the 1099 information as it appears on forms W-9s submitted to you, you must send out *First B-notice (Back-Up withholding notice)* within 15 business days from your receipt of the Notice CP-2100A. The B-notice informs payee(s) that you are required to begin a backup withholding at a rate of 24%

(the withheld tax is remitted to the IRS using the EFTPS processing and reported to the IRS on form 945). Ordered by the IRS action requires you to withhold the backup tax. But earlier the notice says that "you may need to update your records or begin backup withholding." This means that in case that you have your records corrected by mean of internal review or updated W-9 submission, there will be no need to withhold the 24% tax.

The payees to whom you mail the B-Notice must send you updated forms W-9. So, the B-Notice is the Back-Up Withholding Notice that <u>you</u> send out to your payees with IRS-reported tax ID-name discrepancies.

A payee is more likely to respond if you have ongoing payment relationships. There may be one-time payees, whom you had paid in the past and whose names appeared on the Notice CP-2100A who may never replay back to you, because they do not want to provide you correct tax information or just don't care to respond. On the other hand, there are many business and individuals who will immediately send you the required information. Keep in mind that you cannot update the tax ID information over the phone, according to the IRS' instructions.

As soon as you receive Notice CP-2100A, you should put all listed thereon payees *on AP-hold*. That means that from that day on you <u>must not</u> inadvertently make another payment to any payee on the list without first correcting their tax information (or withholding the 24% tax). And payees, understandingly, are much more willing to provide you the requested information if there are held, pending an updated form W-9 receipt, payments.

Before I send a second B-notice out, I add the backup withholding percentage (24%) to those payees' setup who did not respond to me, release the payees' ID from hold and make a note of the IRS notice in the payees' ID reference field. By this time, you should have all those who responded released from hold and non-responders off hold with the tax rate assigned.

The *B-Notice* is supposed to be a straight-forward process, but like many other seemingly simple processes in the accounts payable it can become complicated where you least expect it. I had had a person on the IRS notice CP-2100A with whom my company had an ongoing business relationship, he was providing and billing for the services and we were paying. I sent out a letter asking for update of the W-9 information. The W-9 was returned with the same information as before. I contacted the person again – same results. I then asked to send me a copy of the social security card. Why did I do it and not just keep the signed W-9 on file? The new reportable amount was quite substantial, and I did not want to report it with the same 'bad' SSN (or name), being flagged by the IRS as erroneous.

There were many payments made after the October 24th notice date – I could not use an excuse that the payments were made before the notice was received. And you do not want to be questioned by the IRS even if you have done it all right. I received a copy of the person's SSN. Lo and behold there was another name between first and last names used by the person. This is where the TIN matching system comes in so handy – I could only figure this situation with the help of the IRS's matching tool. I insisted on seeing the SSN card because I was not being able to match the person's W-9 data. The middle name, never used by the person, was the first part of the person's last name, according to the IRS records.

Correction of tax IDs, being the first "action", the second one is "requesting the TIN" if payee's TIN is missing from your records all together. This should not be the case for any orderly accounts payable operation. You must have tax IDs on file for all payees. Now, most of the AP systems "flag" the missing or incorrectly structured tax IDs and do not allow for 1099 processing if a tax ID is missing or formatted incorrectly. I have suggested to my IT team to add a function to our ERP system when each tax ID is checked against the tax name, based on my access to the IRS TIN-matching system. I do not know of any ERP that currently does this kind of IRS-linked matching within the system. A long shot, still 'work in progress'.

Keep track of all B-Notices that you mail out and payees' responses. Update the AP records and assign the 24% tax to the non-responders. Make sure that the assigned tax is not removed by another AP system' authorized user.

In year 2016 the IRS made the B-Notice process a little easier for an unlikely situation that are you paying a vendor with a B-Notice, still have no correct EIN on file, and collecting the 24% back up withholding. The rule is called "2nd Tin not." – see a quote from the 2019 1099-MISC Instructions on it:

You may enter an "X" in this box if you were notified by the IRS twice within 3 calendar years that the payee provided an incorrect taxpayer identification number (TIN). If you mark this box, the IRS will not send you any further notices about this account.

However, if you received both IRS notices in the same year, or if you received them in different years but they both related to information returns filed for the same year, do not check the box at this time. For purposes of the two-notices-in-3-years rule, you are considered to have received one notice and you are not required to send a second "B" notice to the taxpayer on receipt of the second notice.

I advise that you do not use the 2nd TIN Not rule – it is a sign of a less compliant AP process and may invite an IRS audit of your department.

The end of the CP-2100A process involves having all payees on the IRS notice either corrected or set up with the 24% back up withholding tax.

Combined Federal/State (CF/SF) Filing program

To improve the income tax compliance and reporting on the state level the IRS established Combined Federal/State Filing (CF/SF) Program to report all federally reported 1099 income to the participating states (not all states participate), synchronize federal and state tax reporting and, last, simplify information returns filing for the taxpayer. IRS will forward original and corrected information returns (participating forms 1099, 1099-MISC is included in the program) to participating states (see listing of participating states below) free of charge for approved filers. Separate reporting to those states is not necessary.

A third party 1099 consultant will file with the states where necessary. The already mentioned www.tax1099.com does it for me and indicates who gets, as required, filing done with the state.

Systems Transitions and Upgrades

A commonplace process that many AP departments have gone through recently or plan for is a system upgrade process. Our times demand a more effective, efficient, and real-time customer service attuned to the financial processes that can no longer be supported by the old accounting systems.

The ERP systems allow two-way 24/7 interactions with vendors, customers, and other external and internal users, internal controls and processing workflows that both speed up and improve the quality of the financial processing and reporting and availability of the supporting documentation in electronic formats that is available from within the system.

In the ERP system that I use I have immediate access to payees W-9s and bank account information forms that are attached to the payees' master records. An e-mail may be attached to a journal entry to justify its processing or approval. Images of Purchase Requisition, Purchase Order, Receiving Report, and Invoice are attached to the respective AP records as e-documents. Many a time an image is not required to begin with, since all the processing and authorizations were initiated and approved within the same system (e.g. Purchase Requisition, Purchase Order, and Receiving Report). Built-in internal control rules and segregation of duties assure that processing and approvals runs along the predetermined 'check points' that provide for separation of authorization, recording, and custody of transactions and records.

Using an ERP system has become the 'new normal' and the expected level of technical wherewithal for most of mid- to large-size businesses. Companies shop around for ERP systems and buy what they desire and can afford from SAP, Oracle, Microsoft, and other vendors.

The conversion process can span years of analysis, design, specifications, planning, implementation, and parallel run of the old and new systems. The AP process as it has been run in the old system often does not fully reference (or map) to the new system processes. In actual fact, the old system algorithms match only a small number of the ERP systems processes. Many of the AP procedures must be analyzed, assessed, and further developed to assure efficient processing, reporting and compliance utilizing the new system. It is a good opportunity to update and upgrade the existing AP processes and procedures.

1099 processing procedures are often rewritten for the new system's processes. Initially, there is a good deal of inertia and resistance to the new system's logic and demands, and I have experienced this myself. The transition often involves using both, new and old, systems simultaneously; one reason may be a safety parallel processing that backs up the new system's operations. Another is a timing reason; for example, all checks to void that were processed in the old system must be processed in the new system with journal entries, since there are no old checks in the new system, but only the beginning accounts balances.

My old legacy system (called *Computron*, used in the old days by Pfizer and A&E television networks, among others) had 1099 reporting codes specified in payees' master records. But the voucher entry process also allowed for 1099 codes overwriting. The old process allowed exclusion of a reimbursement for a New Year party cake paid to a royalty recipient, as one real life example. My new ERP system does not allow such payment modification. The ERP system requires adjustment of the 1099 amounts if there is such need. The seeming lesser flexibility of the ERP process is a good control that prevents the overwriting of the payees 1099 codes. Do we end up with a New Year party cake reimbursement on form 1099?! It is not a perfect world; as I said before, the 1099 process is a tedious process no matter what accounting system is used. Besides, the ERP system may select vendors and amounts for reporting based on the GL codes.

With the great prospects of having a new system in place, there may appear several unexpected interdepartmental interactions issues. During the system transition that I have gone through I observed certain inter-office political power re-adjustments; the IT department, responsible for the new system customizing and implementation, quite logically *got strong* and influential. IT managers, none of whom were finance or accounting professionals, were instructing the finance department on the financial processes based on the new system's design and abilities.

There was a bit of the "cart in front of the horse" situation because the accountants were told by the IT personnel how to run the accounting affairs based on what the system could do being in the 'out-of-the-box' shape. One advice that sounded more like a demand from the IT was not to use any information for the invoice number field in cases where there is no invoice number *per se*. The new system allows the *blanks* for the invoice number filed. Later, I had to struggle during the 1099 review with thousands of invoice records that had no readily available invoice numbers (or rather invoice references in the invoice number fields) that were foregone based on the IT's blank invoice numbers suggestion (such references are usually made up by AP processors, "trip to Amherst, MA", "taxicab/NASA meeting" or "Honorarium, 12-29-2014"), and serve a much better purpose than a blank space. There is a controversial element in the transition process, and I wish that your finance department is strong enough in your company's hierarchy to demand and assume a full control of the financial processes establishment within the new system.

The new system must be initially run in the test mode. Then a production is rolled out to a limited segment of business, usually the most controlled cost center or department and the new system is run in parallel with the old one to avoid any possible data loss. Once the confidence that the new system is fully operational on the company-wide level is gained, it is released to all cost centers or departments and, again, is run in the 'parallel' mode for 6 to 12 months.

The system should be closely monitored, and many adjustments will be made to the 'live' system already in use. It is a reality that one cannot fully develop a new system in the test mode unless it is a very simple system. The ERP's are not simple systems and fine-tuning and fixing of unexpected issues continues in the production phase. As I have mentioned earlier, it is a prudent process to upload the information processed in the new system back to the old system on a daily (nightly) basis in case of a major unforeseen contingency that may render the new system inoperable.

Epilogue

The 1099 compliance is a tough task to manage. You rarely get praises for a quality 1099 processing. Let me change that – you never get noted for completing the laborious 1099 project on time. *Set la vie.* You may be asked, but not praised. Well, I never was.

No one will call you to thank for the 1099 received after they are mailed out. And you sure get chided for any 1099 reported flaws.

It is a matter of fact statement or, worse, a reminder to your last year's payees to include the reported funds in their tax returns. Often you will be getting calls from the frustrated 1099 recipients who believe that their incomes are not reportable, or promises had been made to the recipient that no 1099 will be involved, by the departments or offices were the service contracts originated.

There is a new and unwelcome reporting deadline of January 31st to both 1099 recipients and the IRS (NEC). This is a relatively new, year 2016 and after reporting, rule. Time and again, you should not rush the filing with both your recipients and the IRS and wait reasonably, literally until the "last minute". Every new day before the deadline may bring you another correction that you must make before filing with the recipients or the IRS. If your 1099 filing were easy to the point where you do not expect any errors or corrections, you would not read this book to begin with. If you are reading this book, it means that your 1099 is not the "push of a button" process; it requires attention, time, and effort to produce quality in the 1099 processing.

So, why am I so excited about the 1099 compliance? My excitement is a subdued and reserved one. Nobody in my department wants to deal with the 1099s. But the process is crucial to be compliant with the IRS regulations. And I am the one who is responsible for carrying this heavy professional burden. I am quietly proud for covering this complicated, tedious, time consuming and sometimes adversarial and controversial area of tax reporting. I hope that you also have this sense of professional responsibility and pride.

You must know and update your 1099-related expertise to run the process and stand up for the filing results if need be. You must know the 1099 regulations inside-out. You must understand the reasons behind the IRS' 1099-related regulations. Enforcing the 1099 rules and being cognizant of the logic behind them will ensure your professional and courteous 1099 processing and customer service.

I wish you success and happiness in your professional lives and beyond. My God bless you, family, and friends.

Sincerely,

Costa Levi Perepeliza, CPA
New York City, 2022

Appendix

Type of form 1099	Description of form 1099
Form 1099-A	Acquisition or Abandonment of Secured Property (Info Copy Only)
Form 1099-A	Acquisition or Abandonment of Secured Property (Info Copy Only)
Inst 1099-A and 1099-C	Instructions for Forms 1099-A and 1099-C, Acquisition or Abandonment of Secured Property and Cancellation of Debt
Inst 1099-A and 1099-C	Instructions for Forms 1099-A and 1099-C, Acquisition or Abandonment of Secured Property and Cancellation of Debt
Form 1099-B	Proceeds from Broker and Barter Exchange Transactions (Info Copy Only)
Form 1099-B	Proceeds from Broker and Barter Exchange Transactions (Info Copy Only)
Inst 1099-B	Instructions for Form 1099-B, Proceeds from Broker and Barter Exchange Transactions
Inst 1099-B	Instructions for Form 1099-B, Proceeds from Broker and Barter Exchange Transactions
Form 1099-C	Cancellation of Debt (Info Copy Only)
Form 1099-C	Cancellation of Debt (Info Copy Only)
Form 1099-CAP	Changes in Corporate Control and Capital Structure (Info Copy Only)
Form 1099-CAP	Changes in Corporate Control and Capital Structure (Info Copy Only)
Inst 1099-CAP	Instructions for Form 1099-CAP
Inst 1099-CAP	Instructions for Form 1099-CAP, Changes in Corporate Control and Capital Structure
Form 1099-DIV	Dividends and Distributions (Info Copy Only)
Form 1099-DIV	Dividends and Distributions (Info Copy Only)
Inst 1099-DIV	Instructions for Form 1099-DIV, Dividends and Distributions
Inst 1099-DIV	Instructions for Form 1099-DIV
Form 1099-G	Certain Government Payments (Info Copy Only)
Form 1099-G	Certain Government Payments (Info Copy Only)
Inst 1099-G	Instructions for Form 1099-G, Certain Government Payments
Inst 1099-G	Instructions for Form 1099-G, Certain Government Payments
Form 1099-H	Health Coverage Tax Credit (HCTC) Advance Payments (Info Copy Only)
Form 1099-H	Health Coverage Tax Credit (HCTC) Advance Payments (Info Copy Only)
Inst 1099-H	Instructions for Form 1099-H, Health Coverage Tax Credit (HCTC) Advance Payments

Inst 1099-H	Instructions for Form 1099-H, Health Coverage Tax Credit (HCTC) Advance Payments
Form 1099-INT	Interest Income (Info Copy Only)
Form 1099-INT	Interest Income (Info Copy Only)
Inst 1099-INT and 1099-OID	Instructions for Forms 1099-INT and 1099-OID, Interest Income and Original Issue Discount
Form 1099-K	Payment Card and Third Party Network Transactions
Inst 1099-K	Instructions for Form 1099-K, Payment Card and Third Party Network Transactions
Form 1099-LTC	Long Term Care and Accelerated Death Benefits (Info Copy Only)
Form 1099-LTC	Long Term Care and Accelerated Death Benefits (Info Copy Only)
Inst 1099-LTC	Instructions for Form 1099-LTC, Long Term Care and Accelerated Death Benefits
Inst 1099-LTC	Instructions for Form 1099-LTC, Long Term Care and Accelerated Death Benefits
Form 1099-NEC	Nonemployee compensation reporting
Form 1099-MISC	Miscellaneous Income (Info Copy Only)
Inst 1099-MISC	Instructions for Form 1099-MISC, Miscellaneous Income
Inst 1099-MISC	Instructions for Form 1099-MISC, Miscellaneous Income
Form 1099-OID	Original Issue Discount (Info Copy Only)
Form 1099-OID	Original Issue Discount (Info Copy Only)
Form 1099-PATR	Taxable Distributions Received From Cooperatives (Info Copy Only)
Form 1099-PATR	Taxable Distributions Received From Cooperatives (Info Copy Only)
Inst 1099-PATR	Instructions for Form 1099-PATR, Taxable Distributions Received From Cooperatives
Inst 1099-PATR	Instructions for Form 1099-PATR, Taxable Distributions Received From Cooperatives
Form 1099-Q	Payments From Qualified Education Programs (Under Sections 529 and 530) (Info Copy Only)
Form 1099-Q	Payments from Qualified Education Programs (Under Sections 529 and 530) (Info Copy Only)
Inst 1099-Q	Instructions for Form 1099-Q, Payments from Qualified Education Programs
Inst 1099-Q	Instructions for Form 1099-Q, Payments from Qualified Education Programs
Form 1099-R	Distributions From Pensions, Annuities, Retirement or Profit-Sharing Plans, IRAs, Insurance Contracts, etc. (Info Copy Only)

Form 1099-R	Distributions From Pensions, Annuities, Retirement or
Form 1099-R	Profit-Sharing Plans, IRAs, Insurance Contracts, etc. (Info Copy Only)
Inst 1099-R and 5498	Instructions for Forms 1099-R and 5498, Distributions From Pensions, Annuities, Retirement or Profit-Sharing Plans, IRAs, Insurance Contracts, etc. and IRA Contribution Information
Inst 1099-R and 5498	Instructions for Forms 1099-R and 5498, Distributions From Pensions, Annuities, Retirement or Profit-Sharing Plans, IRAs, Insurance Contracts, etc. and IRA Contribution Information
Form 1099-S	Proceeds from Real Estate Transactions (Info Copy Only)
Form 1099-S	Proceeds from Real Estate Transactions (Info Copy Only)
Inst 1099-S	Instructions for Form 1099-S, Proceeds From Real Estate Transactions
Inst 1099-S	Instructions for Form 1099-S, Proceeds From Real Estate Transactions
Form 1099-SA	Distributions From an HSA, Archer MSA, or Medicare Advantage MSA (Info Copy Only)
Form 1099-SA	Distributions From an HSA, Archer MSA, or Medicare+Choice MSA (Info Copy Only)
Inst 1099-SA and 5498-SA	Instructions for Forms 1099-SA and 5498-SA, Distributions From an HSA, Archer MSA, or Medicare Advantage MSA and HSA, Archer MSA, or Medicare Advantage MSA Information

Form **W-9**	**Request for Taxpayer**	Give Form to the
(Rev. October 2018) Department of the Treasury Internal Revenue Service	**Identification Number and Certification** ▶ Go to *www.irs.gov/FormW9* for instructions and the latest information.	requester. Do not send to the IRS.

1 Name (as shown on your income tax return). Name is required on this line; do not leave this line blank.

2 Business name/disregarded entity name, if different from above

Print or type.
See Specific Instructions on page 3.

3 Check appropriate box for federal tax classification of the person whose name is entered on line 1. Check only **one** of the following seven boxes.

☐ Individual/sole proprietor or single-member LLC   ☐ C Corporation   ☐ S Corporation   ☐ Partnership   ☐ Trust/estate

☐ Limited liability company. Enter the tax classification (C=C corporation, S=S corporation, P=Partnership) ▶ _____

Note: Check the appropriate box in the line above for the tax classification of the single-member owner. Do not check LLC if the LLC is classified as a single-member LLC that is disregarded from the owner unless the owner of the LLC is another LLC that is **not** disregarded from the owner for U.S. federal tax purposes. Otherwise, a single-member LLC that is disregarded from the owner should check the appropriate box for the tax classification of its owner.

☐ Other (see instructions) ▶

4 Exemptions (codes apply only to certain entities, not individuals; see instructions on page 3):

Exempt payee code (if any) _____

Exemption from FATCA reporting code (if any) _____

(Applies to accounts maintained outside the U.S.)

5 Address (number, street, and apt. or suite no.) See instructions.

Requester's name and address (optional)

6 City, state, and ZIP code

7 List account number(s) here (optional)

Part I   Taxpayer Identification Number (TIN)

Enter your TIN in the appropriate box. The TIN provided must match the name given on line 1 to avoid backup withholding. For individuals, this is generally your social security number (SSN). However, for a resident alien, sole proprietor, or disregarded entity, see the instructions for Part I, later. For other entities, it is your employer identification number (EIN). If you do not have a number, see *How to get a TIN*, later.

Note: If the account is in more than one name, see the instructions for line 1. Also see *What Name and Number To Give the Requester* for guidelines on whose number to enter.

Social security number

☐☐☐ – ☐☐ – ☐☐☐☐

or

Employer identification number

☐☐ – ☐☐☐☐☐☐☐

Part II   Certification

Under penalties of perjury, I certify that:

1. The number shown on this form is my correct taxpayer identification number (or I am waiting for a number to be issued to me); and
2. I am not subject to backup withholding because: (a) I am exempt from backup withholding, or (b) I have not been notified by the Internal Revenue Service (IRS) that I am subject to backup withholding as a result of a failure to report all interest or dividends, or (c) the IRS has notified me that I am no longer subject to backup withholding; and
3. I am a U.S. citizen or other U.S. person (defined below); and
4. The FATCA code(s) entered on this form (if any) indicating that I am exempt from FATCA reporting is correct.

Certification instructions. You must cross out item 2 above if you have been notified by the IRS that you are currently subject to backup withholding because you have failed to report all interest and dividends on your tax return. For real estate transactions, item 2 does not apply. For mortgage interest paid, acquisition or abandonment of secured property, cancellation of debt, contributions to an individual retirement arrangement (IRA), and generally, payments other than interest and dividends, you are not required to sign the certification, but you must provide your correct TIN. See the instructions for Part II, later.

Sign Here	Signature of U.S. person ▶	Date ▶

7171 ☐ VOID ☐ CORRECTED

PAYER'S name, street address, city or town, state or province, country, ZIP or foreign postal code, and telephone no.	OMB No. 1545-0116	
	Form **1099-NEC**	**Nonemployee Compensation**
	(Rev. January 2022)	
	For calendar year 20___	

PAYER'S TIN	RECIPIENT'S TIN	1 Nonemployee compensation $	**Copy A**
			For Internal Revenue Service Center
RECIPIENT'S name		2 Payer made direct sales totaling $5,000 or more of consumer products to recipient for resale ☐	**File with Form 1096.**
		3	For Privacy Act and Paperwork Reduction Act Notice, see the current General Instructions for Certain Information Returns.
Street address (including apt. no.)		4 Federal income tax withheld $	
City or town, state or province, country, and ZIP or foreign postal code		5 State tax withheld $ / $	6 State/Payer's state no.	7 State income $ / $
Account number (see instructions)	2nd TIN not. ☐			

Form **1099-NEC** (Rev. 1-2022) Cat. No. 72590N www.irs.gov/Form1099NEC Department of the Treasury - Internal Revenue Service

Do Not Cut or Separate Forms on This Page — Do Not Cut or Separate Forms on This Page

Form **1042-S**	Foreign Person's U.S. Source Income Subject to Withholding	**2019**	OMB No. 1545-0096

Department of the Treasury
Internal Revenue Service

▶ Go to *www.irs.gov/Form1042S* for instructions and the latest information.

Copy A for
Internal Revenue Service

UNIQUE FORM IDENTIFIER	AMENDED	AMENDMENT NO.

1 Income code	2 Gross income	3 Chapter indicator. Enter "3" or "4"		13e Recipient's U.S. TIN, if any		13f Ch. 3 status code
		3a Exemption code	4a Exemption code			13g Ch. 4 status code
		3b Tax rate	4b Tax rate	13h Recipient's GIIN	13i Recipient's foreign tax identification number, if any	13j LOB code

5 Withholding allowance	
6 Net income	
7a Federal tax withheld	13k Recipient's account number
7b Check if federal tax withheld was not deposited with the IRS because escrow procedures were applied (see instructions) . . . ☐	13l Recipient's date of birth (YYYYMMDD)
7c Check if withholding occurred in subsequent year with respect to a partnership interest . . . . ☐	
8 Tax withheld by other agents	14a Primary Withholding Agent's Name (if applicable)
9 Overwithheld tax repaid to recipient pursuant to adjustment procedures (see instructions) ( )	14b Primary Withholding Agent's EIN
10 Total withholding credit (combine boxes 7a, 8, and 9)	15 Check if pro-rata basis reporting ☐
11 Tax paid by withholding agent (amounts not withheld) (see instructions)	15a Intermediary or flow-through entity's EIN, if any	15b Ch. 3 status code	15c Ch. 4 status code
	15d Intermediary or flow-through entity's name

12a Withholding agent's EIN	12b Ch. 3 status code	12c Ch. 4 status code

12d Withholding agent's name	15e Intermediary or flow-through entity's GIIN
	15f Country code	15g Foreign tax identification number, if any
12e Withholding agent's Global Intermediary Identification Number (GIIN)	15h Address (number and street)
12f Country code	12g Foreign tax identification number, if any	15i City or town, state or province, country, ZIP or foreign postal code
12h Address (number and street)	16a Payer's name	16b Payer's TIN
12i City or town, state or province, country, ZIP or foreign postal code	16c Payer's GIIN	16d Ch. 3 status code	16e Ch. 4 status code
13a Recipient's name	13b Recipient's country code	17a State income tax withheld	17b Payer's state tax no.	17c Name of state
13c Address (number and street)	
13d City or town, state or province, country, ZIP or foreign postal code	

For Privacy Act and Paperwork Reduction Act Notice, see instructions.

Cat. No. 11386R

Form **1042-S** (2019)

Section 117, Internal Revenue Code

"Qualified" scholarship/fellowship payments, as defined by Internal Revenue Code Section 117, are not included in the student's income for federal income tax purposes and are not subject to federal income tax withholding. For a payment to be considered "qualified," a student (as permitted by the terms under which the payment is made) must use the payment for:

1. tuition and fees required for enrollment or attendance, or

2. fees, books, supplies, and equipment required for courses of instruction.

Scholarship/fellowship payments paid in excess of qualified scholarships (i.e. room and board, travel, dorm charges, etc.) are included in the student's income.

[US students should include the non-qualified portion of scholarship/fellowship receipts in their gross income. This is student's personal tax reporting obligation and responsibility. Such non-qualified payments of scholarship and fellowship grants made to US students are not reported by payer to US students and the IRS. Non-qualified scholarship is reported to the US temporary visitors- nonresident aliens for tax purposes. Costa Levi Perepeliza].

www.ingramcontent.com/pod-product-compliance
Lightning Source LLC
Chambersburg PA
CBHW051219170526
45166CB00005B/1960